Thirst for Truth

FROM MOHAMMAD TO JESUS

NIKKI KINGSLEY

FROM MOHAMMAD TO JESUS

Thirst for Truth
From Mohammad to Jesus

By Nikki Kingsley

ISBN-13: 978-1-942634-62-1

Second Edition

This book may be ordered online at:
www.NikkiKingsley.com

For reasons of privacy, certain names in this book have been changed.

Cover Illustration: Nicole Mele
Interior Layout Design: Ryan Illg
Printed in the United States of America

10 9 8 7 6 5 4

Thirst
for
Truth

FROM MOHAMMAD TO JESUS

DEDICATED TO
THE BLESSED VIRGIN MARY
QUEEN OF PEACE

From Mariam of the Quran to Mary of the Bible, you walked with me through the peaks and valleys of my life. You knew my thirst for truth, and in time, you gently led me to your Son, who is Truth Incarnate. I will be forever grateful for this gift of life, for before Christ, I was dead, and now in Christ I am alive!

Blessed Mother, in this centennial of your appearance in Fatima, I offer this book to you as a token of thanksgiving for leading me to the priceless treasure of Truth. I pray that you touch every heart that reads it, and may they encounter Truth in a profound way that leaves them filled with faith, hope and love.

Praised be your Son, Christ the King.

SPECIAL THANKS TO:

My Grandmother

For being the constant melody of love and wisdom,

My Parents

For introducing me to the love and mystery of God,

My Children

For loving and trusting me through the
difficult steps of our Dance of Life,

My friend Joan Tarca Alix

For her invaluable support in making this book a reality.

TABLE OF CONTENTS

Part 3: LIGHT

FOREWORD

"I went without discerning, and with no other light except for that which in my heart was burning."

– St. John of the Cross

It is easy for one to read an autobiography as a detached spectator permitted into a person's life. Indeed, this is how we read most autobiographies. For example, we might read Anne Frank's *Diary of a Young Girl* with interest into the mind and life of a Jewish teenager trying to cope with Nazi persecution. Or, we might read Ernest Hemingway's *A Movable Feast* to gather insights into the novelist's relationship with his famous friends, as well as his lifelong love of Paris.

Some autobiographies are so much more than an accounting of a person's life. If the reader were to act as a detached spectator, he or she would miss the whole purpose of the author's work. The most obvious example of this is St. Augustine's *Confessions* which challenges the reader to join him in his prayer to God and to consider how the Lord will also write straight with the crooked lines of the reader's life.

Nikki Kingsley's *Thirst for Truth: From Mohammed to Jesus*, calls the reader to take a step away from being a spectator to her life and step in, and consider the ways the Lord is calling him or her to Himself. It is certainly interesting to learn about the workings of a Pakistani Ismaili Muslim family and the demands placed on women even in a more liberal practice of Islam, but there is so much more to this book than a presentation of culture.

Thirst for Truth is ultimately a challenge to the reader to be open to the Presence of the Lord, whether He appears in a dream, in a vision, or simply through an inner drive burning deep within the reader's heart.

Join Nikki as her love of God is transformed from her fear of the detached Allah to her embrace by the loving Abba. Consider how great our Father's love is for each of us. Listen to her to the call of Mary, to find forgiveness and peace in her Son, not just the Prophet Isa, but Jesus, the Son of God. Be open to the Spirit who empowers the faithful to proclaim the love of God to the world.

We are people who are loved, forgiven, and empowered. We find our meaning in life in the name of the Father, Son, and Holy Spirit.,

Read, enjoy, and participate in *Thirst for Truth*.

Msgr. *Joseph A. Pellegrino, Pastor,*
St. Ig*natius of Antioch Parish,*
Tarpon Springs, FL

PROLOGUE

"In the beginning was the Word,

And the Word was with God,

And the Word was God.

He was in the beginning with God.

All things came to be through Him,

And without Him, nothing came to be.

What came to be through Him was life,

And this life was the light of the human race;

The light shines in the darkness,

And the darkness has not overcome it."

– John 1:1-5

What is Life but a dance between Light and Darkness? We enter the ballroom at birth and begin this dance, and how well we master the steps and perform the dance determines where we will live for all eternity. This is the Dance of Life, and the Light should be our destination. But often we spend our time dancing in the arms of Darkness confused, injured, and lost. Such is my story, spent in the embrace of empty Darkness until my Beloved came to save me and guide me into the Light. This is my journey from Mohammad to Jesus.

As I begin my story and lay my life open before you, I do so with the desire that you see the incredible love of God the Father. This heavenly Father never gave up as He saved and salvaged the life of His daughter lost in the complex Dance of Life. As you travel with me through the turns of my life, I hope that you too are left in awe at the depth of love that God has for all His children.

I invite you to follow me back into the Muslim world where religion and culture reigns as a merciless king, and then follow me into the transforming love that made me a new creation. Walk with me through the darkness into the Light.

PART 1

FROM INNOCENCE TO DARKNESS

"All shall be well, all shall be well …
For there is a Force of love moving through the universe that holds us
fast and will never let us go."

— St. Julian of Norwich

NIKKI KINGSLEY

CHAPTER 1

Karachi, Pakistan

"Naylah! Naylah! Don't do this to your grandmother. Come out now, child!"

I giggled, trying to stay still behind the curtain as I heard Maji's voice get closer.

"Naylah, I am going to tell your parents what you do to your old grandmother when they are gone! I will tell them this time, I promise you!" Maji was in her sixties, a small and slender woman, and definitely not an old grandmother as she was calling out to me. She was, in fact, an energetic and sharp woman who had overcome many adversities in her life.

I couldn't keep still anymore and fell out giggling and laughing from behind the curtain, falling right at Maji's feet. She saw me, and the frustration was soon replaced by a look of tender love and she sat on the floor, laughing with me as I snuggled in her arms. At four years old, my life was full of simple joys. As Maji gently tucked me in bed and caressed my head, I grabbed her hand and begged her for a story. Maji loved to tell the stories she had learned from her grandmother, so she settled comfortably on the bed and started the story of Sonbai, a beautiful young girl who was tortured by her stepmother and stepsisters, and how she would hear her dead mother singing to her when the wind blew through the trees. Maji would sing the songs, and her voice was full of emotions that would transport me into the story. Of course, there was a happy ending, and I fell asleep smiling, happy that Sonbai's horrible stepmother and stepsister were kicked out by her father.

Maji was from Bombay, India, and she was an incredibly wise, strong, and graceful woman. Her life had been lonely and challenging, as my grandfather was often absent when the boys were young, that left Maji to raise her five sons on her own with help from her parents. She had a fourth-grade education, and spoke only Gujrati, her native language, but she was determined that her sons get an English education. She was wise enough to know that if they didn't, they would never rise out of poverty.

To make sure that they had every opportunity, she visited the best private schools and begged the principal for a reduced tuition. She was persistent, and eventually she managed to get her sons into the best English schools. She was a woman much ahead of her time and culture!

Maji had also experienced the independence of India from the British and lived through the blood-soaked partition of India, in 1947, as it split into Hindu-majority India and Muslim-majority Pakistan. She fled the violent Hindu-Muslim riots with her family and went to the newly-formed Pakistan. She was Muslim belonging to the Shia Ismaili sect.

Within Islam there are two major sects, Shia and Sunni. The division occurred after Prophet Mohammad's death over the disagreement on the successor. The ones who picked Ali from Mohammad's lineage were called Shia, and the ones who picked Caliph Abu Bakr, the closest friend of the Prophet, were called Sunni. Over the years many further divisions happened, leading to the Shia Ismaili sect which was the religion of Maji and her family. In the

Ismaili faith, there was no requirement for women to wear the *hijab* (the traditional Muslim head covering). There was no strict segregation between men and women, and many more liberal viewpoints existed that differed from the other Muslim sects.

Maji settled in Pakistan after leaving India with her boys and her husband, who had finally rejoined his family, and they started a new life. Maji's sacrifice and strength paid off as all her sons received an English education and went on to achieve college degrees. Two sons became business owners, another son became a surgeon and moved to England, my father Nazir became an accountant, and the youngest son Aslam entered medical school. Maji celebrated two of her oldest sons' weddings and was finally enjoying the fruits of her perseverance and fortitude.

At this time my parents, Nazir and Zeenat, met in Karachi, the bustling port city of Pakistan. They happened to be neighbors and fell in love at first sight like something out of a romance novel. Pakistan was a Muslim country, and religion defined every aspect of culture and society, and though they both belonged to the liberal Ismaili religion, dating was still not allowed. So the romance blossomed with shy smiles and quick hidden glances on Fridays at the mosque.

Nazir told Maji that he had chosen his bride, and she was pleased with his choice, as my mother Zeenat was beautiful and belonged to a well-respected family. Maji approached Zeenat's family with a proposal for her son, and they happily agreed as Maji's sons were also well-respected men. In 1968 Maji celebrated the wedding of another son and happily welcomed Zeenat into her home. In the Muslim culture it is customary for sons to live with their family after marriage and to support them financially. Zeenat understood the culture and its responsibilities well, and she dutifully adopted the responsibilities of a devoted wife and daughter-in-law. She loved Maji as her mother and slowly a relationship of love and respect started to take root.

A year later, on a brisk December afternoon, I arrived in the world into a loving family. My mother named me Naylah. I had inherited her features, including her unusual green eyes. My parents were delighted to have a daughter, and Maji was overjoyed to finally have a baby girl to spoil. I was spoiled thoroughly by everyone, and when I was four, my twin sisters Zara and Maira joined the family. Along with the housework, my mother's life became extremely busy taking care of me, the newborn twins, and the rest of the family. Life was simple and filled with an abundance of love and joy.

Shortly after my sisters were born, my grandfather passed away, and my father's responsibility grew, especially for Maji whom he loved dearly. As things became more difficult financially with a growing family, and the medical school tuition for Uncle Aslam, whom he wanted to support, my father started looking for better opportunities abroad. He refused to supplement his income with the bribes he was offered to manipulate accounts, a practice commonplace in Pakistan. My father was a man of principle and refused to do anything unethical. Although he resisted, he eventually began to feel cornered as the financial pressure increased and the needs of the family grew.

Afraid he might be tempted out of necessity to compromise his principles, he urgently searched for a job outside of Pakistan. Fortunately, he was offered a job in Tanzania. Since there was an international school that my sisters and I could attend and a large Ismaili population in Dar-es-Salaam, the capital city where we would live, my father accepted the job. Uncle Aslam would be busy with medical school, so the family decided that Maji should join us in Tanzania.

In 1972, my parents with their three daughters and Maji boarded the flight to Dar-es-Salaam, Tanzania, which continued the simple and blissful time for our family.

Oh, how beautiful the music of life, the refrain, this time of wonderful memories being made as we danced together in peace and harmony.

CHAPTER 2

Africa

We moved into an apartment on Ocean Drive, right across from the Indian Ocean, and adjusted easily to the life in Dar-es-Salaam. Soon after moving we met our dear Tanzanian neighbor, Uncle Ayoob and his family, who soon became an extension of ours. They lived on the first-floor apartment and had three grown children. Uncle Ayoob had an Arab mother and an African father, and he spoke six languages including Urdu, our native language, and Gujarati which was Maji's native language.

Aunty Ayoob was an incredible cook and made the best Indian food we had ever tasted. She started her curry in the morning, taking her time with all the fresh ingredients and soon the delicious aromas would waft up and into our apartment window tickling our appetites.

By 7:00 PM, dinner was on the table and often their daughter, who we affectionately called "Dada" which is Swahili for "sister," would come to tell us Uncle was waiting to have dinner together. We happily ran downstairs taking our dinner along to share with them following the aroma to the heavenly curry on the table.

Uncle Ayoob loved to have friends at the table, and Aunty always cooked enough to feed another family, so this was a regular occurrence. Uncle Ayoob, a talented artist, created sketches of us, especially on our birthdays, along with a hat designed by him that we wore proudly. We couldn't have found a better place to live than being neighbors of this kind and welcoming family.

Dar-es-Salaam (shortened by residents to "Dar") had a large expatriate community, diplomats and people employed at various international organizations who socialized together. We met people of different nationalities spanning the globe, and it was refreshing to see the way everyone was respectful and accepting of each other's cultures. We never tried to deny the obvious; we were diverse in color, culture, language, and religion. My sisters and I attended the international school which was mainly full of children from the expatriate community, and though we were shy girls, we adjusted and settled in quickly at the school.

My parents continued to be people who loved and feared Allah and followed the teaching of their Ismaili faith. They assimilated into the society and embraced the international culture in Dar-es-Salaam. Attending the Ismaili mosque every Friday evening allowed us to meet many people. Since men and women both attended the mosque, there were social activities where everyone could freely mingle after prayers. To young girls, the mosque was more of a social place than a religious one.

In addition, we attended functions at the Pakistani Embassy with diplomats from all over the world. There were no televisions in the homes, so the main entertainment was parties and weekly movies at the United Nations compound. My parents soon found themselves immersed in a busy social life, and my sisters and I spent much of our time with Maji and Uncle Ayoob's family.

Soon after moving to Dar I became friends with Ahsan, a boy who was a year older than me and attended the same school; our parents were friends. His father was a brigadier in the Pakistani Army and stationed in Dar. Ahsan was a skinny, buck-toothed eight-year-old boy with kind and gentle eyes. I was timid and shy and didn't make friends quickly. Ahsan's kind and caring ways made me comfortable, and we were soon best friends. To my young eyes, he resembled a knight in shining armor, always watching over me. I never felt lonely when he was around.

One day, while at school, we were scheduled to receive immunization shots, and I was filled with fear. Sobbing, I refused to go to the nurse. Someone got Ahsan out of class, and he came to reassure, and hold my hand while I got the shot! Our friendship was pure and innocent, and he was truly my best friend. It helped that our parents were also close so we were often together. Ahsan was my guardian angel, and we were inseparable.

Sundays were enjoyable, especially since we lived across the street from the beach. Here vendors sold food and throngs of people would picnic. Many of our friends came to our house, and then we ran across the street to the beach to play and buy grilled plantains, sugar cane, and fresh coconut, among other treats. At night, I recall being lulled to sleep by the sound of the waves and the gentle ocean breeze through the large windows of my room. Life in Dar for the next six years was happy and harmonious.

A few years after we moved to Dar, my father's youngest brother, Uncle Aslam, completed his medical school and residency in Karachi and was a physician. We would visit Karachi every year in the summer, and during one of those trips we attended Uncle Aslam's wedding. He married my mother's younger sister Naseem. A marriage between families was not uncommon in our culture and was considered a blessing as it would draw the families even closer.

Maji was happy since she and my mother shared a close and loving relationship, and she was glad to get another daughter-in-law from my mother's family. The wedding was especially festive as both sides were part of our growing family. We returned to Dar two months later, worn out and a few pounds heavier and with the henna, a sign of celebration in the Muslim culture, barely fading.

Shortly after our trip to Pakistan, my father learned about an opening at a hospital in Dar, and he considered it the perfect opportunity for Uncle Aslam. By this time, we had a baby cousin, Farhan, and Uncle Aslam decided to accept the position. He moved to Dar with his family, and we all lived together once again. However, this time it was in a cozy, two-bedroom apartment. My parents and my four-year-old twin sisters shared one room, and Uncle, Aunty, and their baby slept in the other. Maji and I slept on the pull-out sofa in the living room. Sacrifice for family was an integral part of our life, and our family continued to grow closer as Maji watched happily.

A few years later, Uncle Aslam decided to move to England with his family. Not long after, my father accepted a job in Mogadishu, Somalia, and we started to pack and prepare to move. I was heartbroken to leave Ahsan. Knowing our parents weren't going to indulge us with expensive, long-distance phone calls, with tearful goodbyes we parted ways. I soon learned that was just the beginning of many farewells and partner changes in the Dance of Life, since we moved many times over the next twenty years.

I was dancing to the wonderful African beat and joyful melody. My partner was my protector—he danced almost hovering around me, making sure there were no missteps. I felt safe and cared for until we were torn apart—never to see each other again, and the music stilled as I walked off the dance floor.

Mogadishu, Somalia

In Mogadishu, we once again lived on the shores of the Indian Ocean, enjoying the cool breeze, the soothing waves, and the beautiful view. It was a city with a lazy and peaceful feel, and walking everywhere was common and safe. The Somalis were just as friendly as the Tanzanians, and we settled in, although we missed Uncle Ayoob and his family.

As the school year began, I desperately missed Ahsan's friendship which had kept me from feeling alone. I was still shy and quiet. Making friends was a slow process, and beginning all over again in a new school was difficult for my sisters as well. However, they were lucky to at least have each other's company. The major disadvantage of our nomadic life was the inability to form deep, long-lasting relationships. Aware that we would eventually leave compounded the situation and ensured we never became too attached to places or people. It was inevitable that one day we would say goodbye, but thanks to our young age, we could eventually start over and live in the moment.

Life was uncomplicated and even simpler in Mogadishu, and we still didn't have a television or telephone at home. Without these distractions, I became an avid reader. Since there were no bookstores in town, the only resource was the school library, and soon I read all of the Enid Blyton, Nancy Drew, Hardy Boys, Judy Blume, and Agatha Christie books. Romances became my obsession as I entered my teens, and soon I was devouring Mills and Boon and Harlequin romances. My parents were happy to see my interest in reading and never discouraged it even when I turned to frivolous romance novels.

The romance books in those days were not explicit, but rather about true love that lasted forever. Surprisingly it did not seem to concern my parents that I was filling my head with stories of love that crossed cultures, religion, and continents, something that was frowned upon by our culture. I could easily read one to two books per day and soon started to run out of books from our limited school library. I truly was addicted to books, and my heart would race when I had new books to read! When my friends returned from vacation, all I was interested in was if they had new books to share. The books became a window into a world I had not experienced, but one I could visit safely from my room in the sleepy city of Mogadishu with the backdrop of the waves playing a gentle melody.

Maji spent most her time with the three of us girls since my parents continued to lead a full social life. She filled and enriched our lives by telling us stories, singing, and educating us in the fine arts of embroidery, sewing, and crocheting. Skillfully weaving life lessons into whatever activity she was teaching us, she helped to instill wisdom into our young minds. She used few words, which were never wasted and always had a purpose. Teaching us by example, we watched the way she handled different situations in a balanced and graceful manner. I don't ever recall her losing her temper or getting upset. She explained that most of the time silence was the best solution, and control of the tongue was critical to enjoying a peaceful and happy home. Throughout the years, she was a crucial and steadfast presence, and a treasure of wisdom we could always turn to. My sisters and I loved her dearly. Maji turned out to be the best gift that we ever received from our parents!

Just as in Dar, Mogadishu had an expatriate community, and we attended some of the activities and parties with our parents. In the Muslim culture, girls are encouraged to be demure and modest, and shyness is a praiseworthy trait. Our parents were not concerned that we were reserved and quiet. In time, we made some friends and settled in, enjoying this simple life. We were busy every weekend with parties, movie nights at the United Nations compound, and many activities at school. Although my sisters and I were happy to go out, we were never the loud ones who were the life of the party.

A smaller city than Dar, Mogadishu had more of a Muslim influence. Since we were the only Shia Ismailis in town we did not find a mosque to attend for Friday evening prayers as a family. Sunni mosques were abundant, but they were only for men. For the first time, I was exposed to Sunni Islam, and my parents slowly started to adopt their practice of religion.

All of my parents' Pakistani friends were Sunni, including the Pakistani Ambassador. This meant that even during parties, when the call to prayer (*azaan*) was heard on the radio or from a nearby mosque, everyone stopped to say the *namaz*, the common Muslim prayer. As Ismailis, our prayer was different from the usual Muslim *namaz*. My parents were uncomfortable in these situations, feeling like outsiders, since they did not know the *namaz* and could not participate.

My parents were simple people, and to them, it was more important to be part of the Muslim community than to focus on the differences between the sects of Islam. As long as they outwardly practiced Islam, the finer details didn't matter, so they focused on the similarities with the Sunni Muslims rather than what was divisive as Shias. They learned the *namaz* and fasted in Ramadan, something else that wasn't required as an Ismaili, and they slowly adapted to the Sunni Muslim culture. My mother also learned to read the Quran in Arabic. As my parents studied and practiced Sunni Islam they didn't involve us, but instead focused on instilling good values, love, and fear of Allah. They believed the details of practice were unnecessary for young children, and didn't want to confuse us—provided we understood we were Muslims. My sisters and I believed the simple approach to religion, and we never felt any pressure to learn anything different.

Every evening at 5:00 PM we gathered together at the dining table for tea, a ritual introduced by the British during their time in

India, which had become an integral part of Indian culture. This was a relaxed time with our parents who had just awakened, refreshed from their afternoon nap and ready to listen to our stories about school.

It was here, over tea and snacks that we learned life lessons: things such as being a kind and loving person and always pleasing Allah. It was easily our favorite time since we had our parents' full attention, in addition to enjoying my mother's delicious home-baked bread and cookies. We listened and shared our day with them and talked about the upcoming parties and movie nights.

In the summer, when we visited Karachi we would attend the Ismaili mosque, as usual—innocently believing that the differences within Islam were inconsequential. We witnessed how easily our parents floated between the Muslim sects, and we came to believe that being a good, God-fearing Muslim was more important than the rituals and rules of the different Muslim sects. It wasn't important if we were Shia or Sunni—if we believed in the Prophet Mohammad, the oneness of God, and that Islam was the true way. We had an untainted understanding of the Muslim religion.

Unfortunately, this didn't prepare us for the real world, the real truth about the faith, and the strong differences that continued to cause bloodshed. My knowledge of Islam was limited. I never read the Quran, hadith, or the history of Islam, therefore I did not understand the division between Shias and Sunnis, nor did I understand any of the other world religions. Our conversations centered on doing the right thing, sacrifice, and charity. My sisters and I were taught to act selflessly, caring for others before thinking about ourselves. With this simple explanation, I was blissfully skating on the surface of Islam, unaware of what lay beneath the ice. I believed Islam was the only perfect lake (faith) in the world. As I skated off, I trusted the faith of my parents and believed I was on safe ground.

During our summers in Pakistan, we spent our time visiting our large family, speaking Urdu and eating the traditional foods we missed, while Mother would be busy shopping with her sisters. We were always excited when we were allowed to accompany her to the bazaars. Here we shopped for spices, clothes, jewelry, and gifts for friends back in Mogadishu. Soon the excitement would fade because of the unpleasant pinching and groping by men in the crowded bazaars; we were soon ready to leave as we held on to our mother and aunts trying to avoid the men. My mother, accustomed to this type of behavior, accepted it as the ugly part of the shopping experience in crowded bazaars. We were fully covered, at her insistence, and stayed close to her as we hurried from shop to shop, bargaining and haggling over prices.

The best part of summers in Karachi was time with my cousin Amber who was my age and my best friend. She waited in anticipation for me every year; the two of us were inseparable. In those few months, we squeezed in as much fun and conversations as we could, and I ate all the candy and junk food that I couldn't get in Mogadishu.

On Friday, we dressed up to attend the Ismaili mosque. While there, we spent the majority of time giggling as we looked for cute guys! Even as young girls, we realized our purpose and focus was on whom we would marry, that was the objective. Education was secondary until we met our prince. When we married, we knew our goal was to be the best wife and mother. Amber and I lived in the fantasy of carefully-knitted dreams that became embellished by the romance novels I was voraciously reading.

No one attempted to tell us anything different or prepare us for what we would find in the real world as a Muslim wife, which was vastly different from our preconceived ideas. Instead, we grew up in ignorance, and we were left to the mercy of the Muslim world that would take advantage of this innocence and imprison us. That was to be our future. However, for now, Amber and I were enjoying life together, dancing the happy dance of innocent youth.

We enjoyed the summer holidays in Karachi, but by the end of our two-and-a-half-months, my sisters and I were ready to return. We missed our wonderfully free and simple life in Africa where everyone spoke English, we had freedom of dress, and we didn't have to suffer living under the dozens of stifling and restrictive rules related to our behavior. We were happy and excited to return home!

In Mogadishu there was no high school at the American school, so when I completed the eighth grade I enrolled in the British O Level. This was a correspondence course, equivalent to the ninth and tenth grades combined. The work was done independently by mailing assignments back and forth, and the exam center was in Nairobi, Kenya. My mother and I flew there and stayed a week so I could take my final exams.

In the summer of 1982, when Zara and Maira were on summer break, we flew to Indiana to visit Uncle Aslam and Aunty Naseem who were now living in the United States with their two sons, Farhan and Faiz. When they learned there was no high school back in Mogadishu, they invited me to live with them and enroll in a high school in America. My parents approved, as they believed it would be a better education. Though I was nervous, it seemed exciting, and I agreed. They chose Sacred Heart Convent for me, thinking a private, all-girls Catholic school would be better than a secular public school for me. Thankfully they invited Maji to stay as well, since we were close, and she agreed. My parents and sisters returned to Somalia, leaving me to adjust to a complete cultural, emotional and physical transformation of my life.

The happy dance of youth was slowing down as I approached an unknown future in a foreign culture. I tried to listen for the familiar rhythm, but there were too many melodies, and I was lost in the choices.

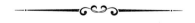

CHAPTER 3

America

The adjustment to America was a difficult transition for me. Everything changed, from the weather to the culture, from the absence of my parents and sisters to the challenge of my teenage years. My life turned upside down, and everything in this new place was suddenly big, fast, and foreign.

The struggle came from the adaptation to Western traditions. Though I attended American schools in Africa my whole life, in America it was vastly different. It was as if I had peered into America through a tiny window with a protective shield; now I walked into a huge and magnified world. Everything from the TV shows, the huge roads, the many restaurants and malls to the beautiful and confident girls at school with their handsome boyfriends who came to pick them up from school. It was a new world, and it was overwhelming for me. It wasn't like Africa where I could just dip my feet in the ocean and return to my safe and familiar home. Instead, I now had to bravely enter the ocean that was America and find a way to stay afloat, having no safe place to run. I was fourteen years old, just becoming aware of my femininity, and here I had entered a whole new world without the familiar and secure presence of my family. Maji was my only constant comfort, but this was a world that was also unfamiliar to her, and she couldn't offer me much guidance. Uncle Aslam was busy with his residency at the hospital and was working long hours and many nights, and Aunty Naseem was busy with her two young boys and seemed disconnected from the fears and confusion of her teenage niece encountering a new culture.

Africa had been a place without many choices and limited information, and I was accustomed to looking at things very simply. Now suddenly there were too many options, from fashion to education, and even the interaction with boys. I had never dated and didn't even consider this an option since it was not acceptable or appropriate in our culture or family. I figuratively "lived romance" through books, but the reality was intimidating and not very appealing. Besides, everything seemed to be the opposite of what I had previously learned. Being obedient to my parents was considered honorable and praiseworthy, but here that was considered a sign of weakness. Telling the truth was very important to me, but these girls were lying and hiding things constantly. My head was spinning with all the contradictions, and I felt ignorant and extremely lonely without my family. I didn't want to make decisions, participate in these activities, or experience such a level of freedom as I didn't know how to handle the consequences.

I was shocked by how complicated my life became, and the realization that I was unprepared to make decisions or choices on my own! Since my parents didn't own a phone in Mogadishu, I had no way of contacting them other than by writing letters. I tried to hide my struggles, putting on a brave appearance for their benefit. My parents would call once a month from my father's office, and it was a short call. I would have a few minutes to say, "Hello," before handing the phone to Maji, Uncle Aslam, and Aunty Naseem. There wasn't time to discuss feelings or struggles.

The one thing that was similar to Mogadishu was that there was no Ismaili mosque in the town, so there was no place to go to worship. There was a small Sunni community, and like my parents, Uncle and Aunty had also adapted to Sunni Islam though they did not pray the *namaz* at home like my parents. They attended the parties within the Pakistani community and the *Eid* festival every year; however they never discussed religion or faith, and this was a time of silence from Islam in my life.

But God was still weaving a path for me to Him though I was completely oblivious. Since I was at a Catholic school, the students were required to go to Mass every Thursday. I had had no education on world religions, and all I knew about Christianity was that it was monotheistic and that the Prophet Jesus was thought to be the Son of God. As a Muslim, I believed that was completely wrong and that Christians were lost, since there was only Allah the Almighty and He had no sons.

This was the one primary teaching my parents had instilled in me. Now I was coming in contact with Jesus for the first time in my life and had no understanding of Him other than the Muslim perspective. Surprisingly, it turned out that no one, including the nuns in this Catholic school, ever spoke to me about Jesus and who He was. I never asked since I was Muslim, and I had no interest in learning about another religion. So, I attended this Catholic school and never heard anyone talk about Jesus or their faith in Him, but I do remember how much peace and love I experienced during Mass every Thursday. This prayer service was different from being at the mosque where I had never felt God's love. I recall realizing how different this was, and wishing that I could feel this love and peace at the mosque. A bonus, here there was a young and handsome priest whom every girl had a crush on!

During lunch, I would sit alone, listening to the conversations swirling around me, amazed to hear girls confidently making decisions for their lives. These girls were dating, thinking independently, and not seeking their parents' approval or permission. I was shocked to learn that they didn't seem to care what their parents thought! I, on the other hand, was raised to make no decisions. Never was I asked about my opinion or thoughts about my life, and all decisions were made for me. I was raised to believe that my parents always knew better.

Now surrounded by these confident girls, I felt embarrassed about myself for the first time. I felt ashamed at my lack of independence and confidence. I was managing the schoolwork, but socially I was a misfit! I felt I had been thrown into a ballet where I was expected to stretch and twirl in ways that my body was not accustomed to, and all around me, the beautiful ballerinas performed the steps with grace and ease while I stumbled around awkwardly.

I tried to act confident at school, but when I came home there was only loneliness waiting, and no one to help me understand this intimidating new world filled with experienced dancers. I began to withdraw to my room and bury myself in schoolwork and my ever-faithful company of books, but even they seemed to have lost their flavor. Most nights I would cry myself to sleep, and many nights Maji would come and comfort me, encouraging me that it would get better. I was overwhelmed and scared. The music had changed, and it seemed I was the only one who didn't know the steps and there was no partner to help guide me.

When winter arrived that year, I saw snow for the first time. It was beautiful to see the spotless white carpet laid out every morning, and I was fascinated by its beauty. In Africa, I had only experienced a hot or cool climate and this "change of seasons" was one experience I enjoyed in America. By Christmas I had two friends at school, so it was a bit better than the first few months of total loneliness. Kim and Rene were both quiet like me and with them I didn't feel a need to act differently. It was a relief to finally not sit alone at lunch every day.

By now I was fifteen years old, and I became aware of my appearance, wanting to look pretty like the other girls. But I didn't know much about makeup and hardly owned any. With this new consciousness came fears and complexes that only compounded my unhappiness. Winter passed and soon I looked forward to the summer holidays when I would see my parents and sisters. Finally, we met in Pakistan, and I was overjoyed to be with them again. I told my mother I was not happy and wanted to return with them to Mogadishu, but my mother told me that I should be strong, urging me to complete a few more years and finish school in America. "Besides," she said, "Uncle and Aunty had been so kind to have you live with them; they would feel bad if you left without completing your schooling." I thought I could do it and didn't want to act weak and disappoint my parents, and since I was obedient, I returned to Indiana in August with a brave face.

Coming back to America was even harder, I missed my family more, and my sadness grew into depression. I started to turn to food for comfort and gained a lot of weight. At the school cafeteria I discovered junk food such as Ding Dongs, chocolate chip cookies, and French fries, which had not been available in Africa.

The weight gain started to affect my self-esteem, and the feeling of being forgotten and isolated grew. I eventually became so despondent that I could hardly get up in the morning and soon this started to affect my school work. I finally talked to my parents and admitted to them I couldn't do it anymore.

Thankfully they decided I should return to Somalia. I was relieved that this painful dance was coming to an end. It was November when Maji and I flew back to my beloved Mogadishu, leaving a disappointed uncle and aunt behind in Indiana.

Little did I know that I had ended this painful ballet a little too soon, for if I had limped through a little while longer, I might have missed a meeting that would lead me into a much longer and excruciating dance that would forever change my life and leave me wounded.

CHAPTER 4

Tahir

Soon after my joyful return to Mogadishu, my parents threw a big party to celebrate my return and my sixteenth birthday. It was on that day filled with laughter that a subtle hint of darkness entered in unnoticed, and I met Tahir. He was the son of my parents' friends, and he was visiting from America during his winter break from college. Tahir was twenty-six years old, studying in America, while his mother was searching for a bride for her only son. I had caught her eye as soon as I had returned from Indiana, and she brought her son to my birthday party so he would have an opportunity to see me.

The usual practice was that parents would show potential brides they had pre-approved for their sons. If the boy liked their choice, he would ask his parents to approach the girl's family with a proposal. Usually the decision was made with no conversation or direct interaction with the girl. While they usually knew the girl, the choice was typically made based on looks. Tahir watched me closely at the party, and over the next two weeks, we met at other events where he came and talked to my friends and me for a few minutes.

My friends and I giggled like the teenagers that we were, as this cute twenty-something guy showed interest in us. There were some older girls who were closer to his age whose parents were desperately hoping that Tahir might be interested in their daughters, and their eyes followed him closely. They could barely cover their anger and frustration as he hardly glanced at their daughters who were trying their best to get his attention with their coy looks, and instead he walked over to the giggling teenage girls! Tahir made his choice, and he let his mother know.

I enjoyed the male attention that was helping to rebuild my wounded self-esteem. The romance novels sprang to life in my mind! Tahir soon left to go back to America, and I eventually forgot about him and settled into my happy life in Mogadishu.

It was a few months later that my father's contract in Mogadishu ended and my parents decided to move back to Pakistan. They thought it would be better for us to settle back in Karachi since my younger sisters were growing up, and soon Zara and Maira would be ready for high school. Girls in the Muslim culture are considered a liability, and parents are eager to get them married quickly to avoid any scandal which would destroy likelihood of proposals from good families. My parents had three daughters, and they thought settling down in Karachi would provide better opportunities for us to get good husbands.

We arrived back in Karachi, happy to have a permanent home and be near our large family whom we always missed. My parents bought a condo near our family, and my sisters started school while I joined St. Joseph's College which, compared to the American standard, is the junior and senior years of high school.

We attended the Ismaili mosque on Fridays with the family, and I began to pay attention to the prayers and teachings. I was sad that I did not hear or feel God's presence at the mosque as my heart longed for Him. Though the moral teachings of the Ismaili faith were good, the main focus seemed to center on material matters and social accomplishments, in other words: worldly success.

There was no real direction on union with God. My spirit was never touched. I didn't gain new spiritual wisdom at the end of the services, though I heard much about worldly wisdom. Deep within me, I was developing a longing for God, a love for Him was budding that created a gentle longing to know Him better and get closer to Him. Unfortunately, I was not receiving instruction or direction that would help me form this relationship, and I would always leave the mosque feeling empty and unfulfilled. My cousin Amber and I would usually be together on Fridays, which was a holiday and we would attend the mosque together. We never discussed faith, but instead this was our social time. She was as much of a romantic as I was and we continued to giggle over cute guys and wondered who would be the hero of our love story.

At school in Karachi, my sisters and I were slowly entering a world that was completely different, and our innocence was peeled away, one layer at a time. It didn't take long for my sisters and me to discover that the education in Pakistan centered around memorization and regurgitation. The expectation was not that the student would understand the concept or theory; the requirement was answering the question exactly, word-for-word from the textbook. If you used your own words, it was considered wrong. The concepts we previously learned throughout our education were totally rejected, and no one was interested in our thoughts or ideas! Plagiarism was not only encouraged, but was the only right answer.

We were amazed at the talent the students in our class had for memorization, something we grappled with! The three of us struggled and would sit through classes completely lost, since many of our lessons were taught in Urdu, the national language that we spoke, but had never studied. They didn't speak the basic Urdu with English words sprinkled in as we did, but rather it was so proper that it sounded like a foreign language to us. Things were a bit easier for me than for my sisters because being in college meant I could skip classes. But unfortunately my sisters, being younger, didn't have that choice. Often my sisters would come home crying with welts on their hands for not getting something right or for not understanding. Physical discipline was allowed in schools in Pakistan again, something we had never experienced.

The education style wasn't the only thing that was a direct opposite of our experience. We were shocked when we realized how rampantly present homosexuality was in both my college and my sisters' school. Our schools were just for girls, and we couldn't help but notice the strange behavior among some of the girls. Exposure to any kind of homosexuality in Africa, among our friends or in school, was never seen and foreign to us. I had never encountered this even in my time in Indiana. It took us a while to even understand what was happening. We quickly realized that the strict rules and religiosity was a façade for many of the girls, and behind it all was an obsession with sex.

We were surrounded by the calls to prayer five times a day in a culture that preached holiness and modesty, and where Islam dictated the law, but we couldn't reconcile the behavior we were witnessing that was in stark contrast to these teachings. We saw a hypocrisy and deception that we had never imagined. We were too embarrassed to bring it up to our parents, and we never discussed it amongst ourselves either. It was only many years later that my sisters and I shared our experiences, and were surprised we had seen the same things transpiring in our schools.

Unbeknownst to us, our parents were also struggling, as the bribery and lying were in all aspects of life in Pakistan. It seemed like no one ever meant what they said, and nothing got done without paying a bribe. There was no respect for the law, as a bribe could get you what you wanted. The rich answered to no one, and the poor were forced to take bribes to survive, and it was nearly impossible to get through a day without encountering a dilemma which would test one's morals. My father tried hard to settle in and start work, but he very quickly realized that nothing had changed but had worsened since he had last lived there.

Shortly after our move to Karachi, Tahir entered my life again. His mother had searched for us in Karachi and had found out where we lived through a mutual friend. One evening the doorbell rang and my parents were surprised to see their friends from Mogadishu at the door with their daughter and trays of sweets.

It was a tradition that proposals were presented with sweets in the hope of a positive answer. Tahir had an older sister Sheena who was devoted to him. Sheena had accompanied her parents, determined to bring good news to her brother, and she promised everything she could to my parents to get them to agree to the proposal. My parents thought it over for a couple of days and discussed it with the family. Surprisingly, my aunts and uncles disagreed with the decision. They had a more liberal outlook compared to my parents, and were shocked that my parents were even considering this proposal.

One disagreement was over our ages; I was too young as I was not even seventeen yet, and Tahir was ten years older than me. A bigger issue was the fact that Tahir was not Shia Ismaili but Sunni, and they thought there would be too many differences between us. Marriage outside the sects was not common and was frowned upon, as each sect was passionate about their beliefs. To my parents, who had lived outside Pakistan and mingled with Sunnis for many years, the differences seemed irrelevant. In Africa, Shias and Sunnis had no problems getting along and my parents didn't see why that would be a problem now. They focused on the fact that Tahir had been raised abroad and had a similar background as me which was more important to them. And after all, he was a Muslim, which according to them was the most-important thing. Against the family's advice, my parents decided to accept the proposal and told me after they made their decision.

Until now there had never been any conversation about my life other than an unsaid understanding that I would go to school as I waited for a good husband. Any plans or dreams centered on getting married, and the romance novels had only helped me stay compliant to this. So, as I sat before my parents that day and heard their decision, I didn't disagree. After all, being a wife was the whole purpose of my life and besides, Tahir was attractive and mysterious. I trusted my parents, and had been raised not to question their wisdom.

Eight months after our first meeting at my party in Mogadishu, Tahir and I were engaged. After spending one evening exchanging a few shy sentences, he flew back to America leaving me to weave a fantasy of undying love with this stranger. A gamble had been taken, and I was too immature to understand the seriousness of the decision that would take me down a treacherous road, forcing me to grow up painfully and abruptly.

Subtly the music started to change its rhythm, but because my heart was pounding in excitement, I failed to notice the movement towards shadows.

A few months after my engagement, my parents finally gave up trying to settle in Karachi. My father received an opportunity to work in Africa again, and we happily packed up and moved to the Congo. The city, Kinshasa, was relatively more developed than Mogadishu, and we now had a television and a telephone at home. There was also as an Ismaili mosque that provided a busy social life and a place to worship every Friday. My sisters and I attended the American school and soon we had happily settled once again in our familiar life in Africa.

Through the two years of my engagement, Tahir and I exchanged postcards and letters, and during a summer break in Florida, we met and spent some time together. Looking back on this time, there were plenty of red flags as his selfishness was obvious, but my young heart was living on innocent dreams woven by the romance novels, and failed to see the cracks. I looked at my engagement as a serious commitment. To me, it was as good as being married, and I believed this was forever and I had no thought of ever breaking it. I was convinced that I could perform the next dance perfectly because I had faith in my partner. I trusted that he would be as committed to performing this number in harmony with me, and with the same goal, we would help each other execute the steps with grace and love.

My sisters and I adjusted without difficulty to life in the Congo versus how we had done in Pakistan. We made friends easily, as we seemed to have much more in common with the kids who lived in Africa. The months flew by, and I neared my high school graduation. All my friends seemed to be focused on plans for college and deciding on their career choices. Suddenly it seemed to me that I was isolated from the discussions. I was the only one who was engaged and going to get married after graduating high school while everyone else was picking colleges all over the world! As I listened to them, I asked myself: What would it be like to go away to college and pursue an education....to dream my personal dreams that didn't involve being dependent on a man and thinking about myself was foreign to me. I had not been encouraged to think about college or personal accomplishments that would make me independent. Now, hearing my friends discuss their dreams and plans, I started to wonder for the first time: What could I be? What were my goals and desires as an individual?

As my friends discussed their dreams and aspirations, I felt a stirring within my heart about discovering the possibilities. I loved school and enjoyed learning, and I realized that I wanted to go to college and that I wanted to explore life more than just being a wife. For the first time, I started to think about myself as an individual and not just as a wife-to-be, and I asked my parents to allow me to get my college degree before I got married. My father told me that since I was engaged, I needed permission from my fiancé and if he agreed then I could pursue college. So, late one night, with my mother by my side and my heart pounding fast with anticipation, I called Tahir in America to ask his permission.

My whole future hung in the hands of a man who was still a stranger to me, but somehow in control of my life. It didn't take him long to say no. He was completely against it as he saw no need for me to get an education since I was not ever going to work. As soon as I heard his answer, I fell over sobbing, dropping the phone. I felt like a window had been opened for me, with light streaming in allowing me to see the world outside, but now suddenly my hands were tied as I watched it get slammed shut, leaving me in darkness.

My mother talked to Tahir and said I would get over it, and I was just excited because my friends were making plans. He told my mother that he wanted to get married as soon as I graduated high school and he got his MBA that summer as planned. I cried for a few days, heartbroken at being ignored and my dreams discarded. I felt like an object passed from one man's possession to another. The decision was made, and there was no further discussion. My parents felt that they and Tahir knew best how to manage my life.

Looking back, I wish I had fought harder, but I lacked confidence in myself and the one bad experience in America further played on my weakness and insecurity, making me nervous about going back to America. My parents thought I was emotional and too young to know better, which only made me doubt my desires. Ironically, I was too young to know better, yet old enough to marry a perfect stranger.

After a few weeks of crying, I accepted the finality of the answer. Maji was aware of the disagreement and my sadness, but she stayed out of the discussion, as she didn't feel she should interfere. Maira and Zara were four years younger than me, and their age gap seemed widened. They were not aware of the seriousness of the decisions that were being made, and were living in their younger, more innocent world of early-teenage years.

I was left on my own to overcome my crushed dreams before I could even create them. My parents and Tahir were now in control of my life, and I had to come to terms with the fact that I had no rights over my identity and my life. I couldn't look further or imagine more than what was allowed. As I watched my friends making plans to leave for different parts of the world to pursue their dreams, I distracted myself with romantic ideas about my marriage and my wonderful knight in shining armor who would love and protect me.

I graduated high school in June 1987, and we traveled back to Pakistan to prepare for my wedding. The first month was spent shopping feverishly for clothes and jewelry as my parents had to prepare the dowry for me, buy gifts for the groom, his family, and our own. Then all the gifts and dowry had to be wrapped beautifully so it could be displayed for all to see before the wedding. What an exhausting and expensive tradition, and my parents did their best to fulfill all of them.

As was the custom, I stayed home for a week before the wedding, and Amber came to stay with me, and she helped stir my romantic dreams! Again, according to custom, there was a whole beauty routine that a bride went through to prepare herself for the wedding, and one of my aunts made arrangements for this. She brought Amma, an old lady who had many years of experience in preparing brides and she was known for her secret beauty concoction. She would scrub my whole body with the special yellow paste for hours every day. By the end of the week, I felt layers of my skin had been scrubbed off, but I had a glow and smelled like roses since she added fresh rose petals to her secret mixture.

As I was going through the beauty rituals, my wedding dress was finished, and the final fittings took place. Amber paraded in and out of the room with different outfits trying to decide what she would wear, while I lay with a mask on my face as Amma vigorously massaged my arms. This was an important occasion for Amber as many matches happened at weddings, and Amber was still single. Mothers looked for potential brides for their sons at the weddings, and the sons tried to make the most of getting a look at the girls so they could discuss the options with their mothers later. Luckily the celebrations lasted at least three days that allowed for discussions and second looks the next day. As Ismailis we didn't wear the *hijab* and neither did Tahir's family, so there would be plenty of opportunity for matchmaking at our wedding.

After a week of intense scrubbing and massaging, Amma's work was completed, and she was ready to move on to the next waiting bride. Three days before the wedding celebration began, my henna was applied, and it took six hours as the woman used a needle to draw the intricate designs on my hands up to my elbow and on my feet all the way to the ankles.

I had to keep the henna on for three days before I could wash it as the longer it stayed on, the darker and prettier the color. During this time, Tahir's family came, as was tradition, to drop off the *bari* which are the gifts from the groom's family. That began the singing and dancing every night as my cousins, aunts, and other women from the family came to help wrap the dowry and to see the *bari*, which would give them a good idea of the wealth and social status of the groom.

Finally, after the three days of singing and dancing, Tahir and I were married, and we moved into his parents' house as was the tradition. Nearly twenty years ago, my mother Zeenat had walked into my father's house and had become part of his family. Today as her daughter, I innocently, and trustingly walked into Tahir's house— but the contrast between our lives was going to be sharp and shocking. The dance that I was led into was starkly different from Zeenat and Nazir's romantic waltz.

Tradition and culture beckoned me away from the excited calls of my friends. I closed my eyes and covered my ears as I turned away, walking into a deceptively simple wedding dance which soon morphed into a complicated dance of manipulation and betrayal.

CHAPTER 5

Darkness

It was shortly after we were married that I really met my husband. One evening, we walked upstairs to our bedroom after dinner with his family, and I mentioned that it would be nice to get a break from the family and for us to have some time alone. For the last two months, we had been surrounded by family, and since we were married we had breakfast, lunch, and dinner with at least fifteen people at the table. I was exhausted of the formality and strain of speaking Urdu all the time. He became extremely angry and started to yell at me, and he was about to hit me when he caught himself. I was shocked and looked at his face, distorted in anger, and my tightly-held love story started to crumble in my hands. I didn't know how to respond, never having witnessed even one disagreement between my parents. My mother was not subservient to my father, but rather they had mutual love and respect. My father treated her with kindness and dignity, just as he did Maji. That was the home environment I came from, so Tahir's harsh tone and anger shocked me. I started to cry, and he walked out, leaving me holding the shattered love story in my hands. This was the beginning of an unhappy marriage in a culture that was ruled by men and a society that was unforgiving and unsympathetic to women.

My parents stayed in Karachi for two weeks after my marriage. I had the opportunity to tell them that things were already bad, but I couldn't. As a married woman, I felt ashamed to complain about my husband, and I felt I needed to build his respect in front of everyone. A complaining wife was considered a reflection on her weak character. I had heard conversations between my parents and Maji when they talked about what was considered honorable and not, and I knew the honorable thing in my situation was to cover up for my husband. I especially remembered this since I had been told many times that I needed to grow up and act mature, so I tried my best to do just that as with my henna-stained hands I hugged my parents, Maji, and my sisters, a tearful goodbye as they left for Kinshasa.

Tahir was an engineer and worked for the government, and he was posted to Hyderabad, a small city in Pakistan. After his two-week vacation was over which we spent with his family, we left for Hyderabad. Living in Karachi was enough of a difficult transition, but Hyderabad was much worse. It was a very conservative city where women wore a *chador*, which was a thick wrap that covered their head and most of the body, and even with that, women were hardly seen outside. Besides, there were frequent lootings and rapes that kept women home.

We lived in the government compound with the military officers, as well as some Americans who worked with the Pakistani government. We had a very basic and modest room with a bathroom and would eat at the dining hall with about 200 other people. Once a week there was a bingo night that was the highlight of the week, and the other nights we could visit with each other or watch movies in our room on a small television.

Within the compound, it was safe for women to move around without the *chador* and only the traditional Pakistani clothes of *shalwar kameez,* which was a long shirt and baggy pants. If I left the compound for any reason to go into the town, I had to cover myself with a *chador,* and even then, I would feel the lustful eyes of the men burning through my clothes, as they watched like wild animals. It brought back the memories of the men grabbing and pinching us in the bazaars, and I shuddered to think how violent they could be if they ever got the freedom to do whatever they wanted to a woman.

I was in shock at the transformation in my lifestyle, and I felt almost numb, unable to comprehend the drastic change in the surrounding culture, the loneliness, and the lack of love. Tahir was a self-centered man with a roving eye and only cared about what he wanted— not unusual for men in my culture, as the traditions and societal laws gave them all the power, and women lived dependent upon them. It was devastating to me, especially since I had never witnessed this kind of marriage. Besides, my parents, my aunts, and uncles also seemed to have loving and respectful relationships. Everything was unfamiliar from where I lived which was far away from my family to the daily etiquettes of my new family.

Slowly the reality was sinking in that this would be my life forever! Tahir's behavior made it clear that he regarded me as his property, and he was not interested in my thoughts, opinions, or desires. I was a wife who was to serve him dutifully, and he would get impatient and frustrated with me when I couldn't act mature and devoted enough to him. He frequently called me childish and crazy, and made it obvious that he didn't care at all if I was lonely or sad. A feeling of abandonment and rejection settled in my heart as I tried to watch movies and escape in the stories to find solace.

Somehow, I survived the six months in Hyderabad until Tahir transferred to Karachi, and we moved in with my in-laws and close to Sheena, my husband's married older sister, which introduced yet another challenge in my life. My in-laws were strict Sunnis and unlike my family, religion dictated and controlled almost everything in their home. My mother-in-law suffered from arthritis and spent most of her day in bed. Since she prayed five times a day and read the Quran daily, her prayer mat was laid out on her bed all day until she went to sleep at night. The prayer times dictated her day, and when she interacted with anyone, her conversations became filled with the teachings of Mohammad and the Islamic rules and Allah's will. What a big change for me as there had been no such conversations and prayer times in my home. Never had my parents ever cited Mohammad's teachings or the Islamic rules.

The food and customs were also foreign to me. The language was very different too, as I spoke an informal style of Urdu with a lot of English words sprinkled in. My in-laws spoke proper Urdu with no English interjections, and I quickly had to learn proper Urdu as I would feel embarrassed by the looks they would give me. Thankfully I had always loved the Urdu language, especially the poetry, and it didn't take long for me to learn it better. My husband and I spoke in English, so I had a small respite from the stress of watching every word and making sure I spoke it correctly.

I also learned the formal etiquettes and graces in their family so as not to shame myself. Over the months, I felt like a child thrown into a grown-up world of cultural do's and don'ts, and a country and society dictated by Islam in which holiness was always on display. However, that hardly ever matched the truth. It seemed like everyone was wearing a mask, and I never knew who I could believe because forthrightness and truth were in severe shortage.

Life settled into a grim and dreary routine with my in-laws. As a daughter-in-law, I was expected to participate in the daily housekeeping activities, and help my mother-in-law manage and oversee the servants. Cooking was not something I had learned growing up. My mother and Maji had prepared the food, and we had a housekeeper who helped them. I had never washed dishes, done laundry, cleaned, or performed any other housework. So now I was a nineteen-year-old married woman, whose face would burn with shame when my mother-in-law asked what I would cook and serve our family for dinner. I couldn't even light the gas stove! I mumbled something about baking a cake once, and hoped she wouldn't ask me to bake one as my role in the process had been to stir the batter! Surprisingly, she smiled, and said she would teach me how to cook. I was oblivious to the fact that she had an unfulfilled desire to be a teacher, and she was thrilled that now she had a full-time pupil!

"Tomorrow after breakfast we will begin your lesson. I will have you cooking all Tahir's favorite dishes in no time. Oh, and bring down the laundry, and I will teach you how to do that as well," she said happily. I thought her excitement about teaching me household duties was a little odd, but I had no idea how seriously she took this teaching opportunity!

The next morning, after I had served my husband his breakfast and he had left for work, I joined my mother-in-law for breakfast, and she went over the menu for the day. The time finally arrived to begin the household duties, and my mother-in-law excitedly stood up, and leaning on her cane, she made her way as fast as she could to the kitchen. She had an eight-year-old servant girl who was her helper, and she had a chair ready in front of the stove for herself. She slowly sat down and began her first lesson: preparing fresh spices for the curry. She taught me the names of the many different spices and their use. She explained that we don't use coriander in most vegetables. She taught the proportion of the spices to use in order so as not to overwhelm the curry, and that certain, freshly-roasted, and ground spices change the flavor of food. And very important was the order in which spices were added to maximize the flavor.

Once we finally had the curry simmering in the final stages, she moved on to the laundry. I separated the laundry under my mother-in-law's watchful eyes, making sure I didn't make a mistake and ruin the clothes. Some of the clothes would be hand washed by a servant and hung out on the line to dry. A chosen few clothes were washed in the treasured, semi-automatic washing machine that didn't drain or spin. I had to weigh these clothes on a weighing scale to make sure we didn't overload the machine, and when washed, the servant would hang them on the line to dry. Then she directed me to follow the other servant who did the cleaning, and check to be sure she didn't miss any corners dusting and sweeping. "They always try to cut corners, so you have to follow and make sure they clean it well. You just can't trust these women who always come asking for money but never want to do the work well!" she told me.

As I followed the woman into the formal living room to oversee the cleaning, I noticed the curry smell wafting from my clothes. Suddenly I felt a painful realization—this was what my life would be from now on: cooking, cleaning, doing laundry and serving my husband and in-laws, and I felt a sob choke in my throat. I felt trapped in prison with a life sentence, and I wondered what my friends were doing in different parts of the world where they had gone to pursue their dreams! How lucky they were, I thought, as I pointed out a missed cobweb to the servant as I tried to hold back the tears.

My mother-in-law took it upon herself to educate me on Islam. She taught me how to wrap the veil correctly so no hair, ears, or arms would show as I presented myself before Allah to pray. I learned the exact position for my hands, feet, and toes when reciting the *namaz*, and to make sure I had no nail polish, as that would be a barrier in the purification ritual before prayers. I studied the long list of things that would make me unclean and how to purify myself for prayer. The holiest day of the week for Muslims is Friday, so Friday and Saturday is considered the weekend in Pakistan. Tahir went to the mosque like most Muslim men to pray the *Jumma*, the Friday afternoon prayer, but that was where his faith ended. He did not read the Quran, fast, or pray any other time. Strangely, he seemed to have an aversion to the Quran.

In contrast, as I learned the Islamic faith and the teachings of Mohammad, I was drawn to all the strict rules. In the Shia Ismaili religion, I had felt a void. It had seemed more of a country club membership than a religion to me, but now I was encountering these rules and teachings which focused on Allah. Since I was so unhappy and felt trapped in an impossible situation from which only Allah could save me, I turned wholeheartedly towards Islam. This dedication drew approving looks from my in-laws and my husband, something I rarely received, so I felt encouraged and prayed more. I hoped that the more faithful I was, the more chance there would be that Allah would favor me with freedom from the living hell I was enduring. I learned all the traditions, rules, rituals, and prayers and I would read the Quran every day and beg Allah to have mercy on me.

The rituals made me feel that coming before Allah was no small matter, and He expected a reverence and fear from me when I prayed. He was the master to be feared for He was also quick to punish. Allah had ninety-nine names that described His attributes, but there was never any hint of a possibility to have a relationship with Him. Rather it seemed that a relationship was impossible, and it was a sin even to desire such a prideful thing as a relationship with the Almighty as that was evidence of pride. The Prophet Mohammad, the perfect man, had a close relationship with Allah and all we needed to do was follow his teaching and actions. I needed an escape, and I pinned all my hope on Allah, and soon I was practicing the Sunni Islam faithfully though I didn't wear the *hijab*, since the Quran only required modesty in dress. Religion had become an escape from the darkness of my life, and a focus on the rules gave me a feeling that I was doing something tangible to be heard by Allah.

Days went by, and a routine started to set in. Mornings were spent doing housework and after lunch things were quiet as the servants left for a break, and my mother-in-law usually took a nap. This was when I could finally escape to my bedroom. Most of the days

I spent crying, depressed and lonely, as Tahir showed a growing detachment and harshness towards me. Eventually, when I had exhausted all my tears, I would gather myself together and sit down to pray. Prostrate on the prayer mat, I begged Allah to release me from this nightmare. My bedroom window had bars on it, and I remember many afternoons looking out, holding the bars, feeling like a prisoner. My heart felt as heavy as lead, as the realization sunk in that this was a true life sentence!

Around 5:00 PM, my husband usually arrived home from work, and we would all gather in the living room for tea. I often thought about the tea time with my parents in Africa and how happy that time was, and what a stark contrast this was. Afternoon tea with Tahir's family was nothing like that joyful time. The servant would bring in the tea-cart to the family room and leave it before me to serve. After the tea steeped, I would serve it with the usual cookies and sandwiches. The television would be on with the news in Urdu, which I could partially understand. Every other word was foreign to me, and the conversations were formal and stilted. Most times my mother-in-law would sprawl out on the carpet in the middle of the family room and moan, rubbing her knee and complaining about the pain.

Typically, her husband and son would ignore her, or look at me, which was the sign for me to massage her knees. I would perform this duty as my husband and father-in-law relaxed with their tea, watching approvingly, while my mind escaped to the joyful tea time with my family in Africa and the taste of my mother's delicious baked goodies. Sometimes we had the opportunity to leave the house without Tahir's parents, and although my relationship with my husband was not great, I was delighted to speak in English and have a reprieve away from the incessant voice of his mother, calling out to the servants and complaining of pain. Financially things were difficult. Tahir earned a modest income, and everything was very expensive. We went out sometimes, but we had to watch our spending carefully, and we definitely couldn't take any vacations. We were dependent on his parents because he couldn't afford to pay for a house himself, which my father-in-law made sure to remind me frequently.

Not only was I in a mental prison, but a physical prison as well. I had no freedom. Since I couldn't drive, I was completely dependent upon my husband or father-in-law. It is difficult to describe the feeling of a world where one person is at the total mercy of another human being's degree of compassion and kindness. It was prison where a woman's identity was kept in invisible chains, destroying all the possibilities of who she could ever be. My husband didn't waste his time on even thinking along these lines and used and discarded me as it suited him. My in-laws never missed an opportunity to remind me that my life and future belonged to them, and my parents understood and agreed with this. My only break from this monotonous and suffocating routine would be my sister-in-law Sheena who, on occasion, would feel sorry for me and take me shopping or out to lunch.

Sheena lived a privileged and independent life. She had a husband who treated her with love and respect, and she had also been blessed with an abundance of money and freedom. She had a car and a driver at her disposal, and she spent most days shopping for her busy social life. My mother-in-law, wanting to make sure I didn't compare my life to her daughter's, quickly clarified to me that her daughter was special and deserved all the privileges she enjoyed, and I shouldn't expect what she had. My life was different she told me, and my job was to serve and take care of them. It was all a matter of *kismet* (destiny). Sheena's *kismet* was better than mine, so she had a wonderful life with all the blessings. My *kismet* was different and I should accept it peacefully.

It wasn't long after I got married that I started to hear conversations within the family about the frequent indulgence in viewing pornography. It became clear that this was a common occurrence. It was shocking for me to realize that pornography was acceptable in an otherwise strict Muslim country. Their rationale was that the people in the films were not Muslim, so there was no need to feel guilty or consider it a sin. Respect was reserved for Muslims, so there was no shame in watching the "infidels" in obscene and coarse movies. I found these conversations shocking and embarrassing, and I tried to process what I was hearing, as the logic sounded irrational.

A deeper level of darkness entered my life, and I could make no sense of the hidden world that existed beneath the holy exterior of this country and people. I couldn't figure out what was right and wrong as the messages were all convoluted. How could nail polish be an obstacle to prayer but porn be completely acceptable? Nothing made sense anymore, and I watched in horror at the ugly world that was unfolding before me.

A couple of my friends from my college days at St. Joseph's lived nearby, yet their lives were very different from mine since they were finishing up their college education. Although they had grown up in Pakistan, they had more freedom to decide their futures, including who they were going to marry. I no longer had much in common with them.

On occasion, I would visit Amber but the distance between our homes was too far, and eventually I saw her only a couple of times a year. When I did visit, I felt disconnected, as my lifestyle had changed so much living in a Sunni home. Soon Amber married and was busy in her life. However, I learned her marriage had turned into a nightmare as well, with her in-laws controlling her life and her husband was as disinterested in her, as mine was with me. Both our lives didn't even remotely resemble our romantic dreams, and where we had once giggled together. It seemed now we had even forgotten to smile. The sadness in our lives separated us, and soon that relationship faded away. My life felt incredibly lonely. I felt abandoned, forgotten by my family and by God, and that my life didn't seem to matter.

It became obvious that Tahir and I had nothing in common and he made no effort to nurture our relationship. His passion was aviation, and it soon became his obsession. He spent hours working on his toy planes. He didn't share his feelings or thoughts and stayed removed from me, knowing that I was his property. He could treat me however he liked, confident I would never leave. Though we were physically living together, we were completely disconnected. My feelings and opinions were of no consequence. Ignored most of the time, I had no choice but to accept my fate. He purposely said things that he knew would hurt me and when he saw me cry, he would smile because that proved to him that he was in control. We would argue every day, and most nights I would cry myself to sleep— hurting, lonely, and filled with fear of my future.

Looking back nearly thirty years later, I can see how similar Tahir was to his father, who also lived an independent life from his wife. My father-in-law was openly flirtatious, and he took great pleasure in using coarse language around women and enjoyed the embarrassed and shocked looks. It seemed he could barely control himself, and I would be nervous at being alone with him, just as were all the women who came to work in the house. I never witnessed such rude, disgusting behavior or language in my life, and most of all I was shocked by the acceptance of these actions by his wife, my husband, and my sister-in-law. My naiveté even kept me blind to his unholy interest in the young eight-year-old servant girl. One day, the girl was abruptly sent back to her family with the claim that she had gone crazy. It is only recently that certain pieces of forgotten memories have re-emerged, to create a picture I would rather not see.

Within my first year of marriage, I discovered I was pregnant. I had no understanding or knowledge of pregnancy symptoms, so was confused by my exhaustion and nausea all day. There was no education of possible symptoms, the effects of pregnancy, or remedies from the doctor; instead, I was diagnosed as pregnant and left to figure out the huge changes happening to my body on my own.

I felt like a child trapped in a grown-up world and had no idea how to deal with the things that were happening. Tahir seemed happy about the baby but irritated by my constant sickness due to the pregnancy, and my father-in-law would laugh at me and call me stupid. My mother-in-law had by now gotten over the teaching phase and started to lose interest in helping, thus she was now short and impatient with me.

I turned to my prayer life with a renewed fervor, one area where I didn't get reprimanded, and even Tahir left me alone. It was believed that reading the *Surah Maryam* (Chapter on Mary) during pregnancy ensured a healthy and holy baby. I loved Maryam, the holy mother of the Prophet Jesus, and I happily read the *Surah* daily and prayed for the baby I was carrying. I felt that by praying, I was actively doing something to fight my situation. I was praying for a miracle.

My daughter Sania was born after midnight in the hot month of July to an exhausted and medicated mother. I returned home from the hospital feeling even more depressed and fearful, since now I had to watch my daughter's life being suffocated in this family and culture. Tahir was excited and happy to be a father, but disinterested in any responsibilities that came with fatherhood. He treated Sania like a toy that he could play with and hand back to me. We never discussed what being parents would involve and any future planning with our new child.

I felt choked with the lack of freedom for myself and for my daughter's future. I didn't want her to have this kind of life. I at least had had a good childhood in a better environment; she would be squashed right from birth! In my heart I knew that everything was wrong, and it wasn't supposed to be the way it was, though the society around me told me this was normal. I turned towards Allah in desperation, and I started praying even more desperately, begging for a miracle for Sania and me. I was trying to be as faithful to my faith as possible, hoping that Allah would take pity on me and save me. Deep in my heart, I believed God was a God of love and mercy, but I couldn't understand why He had left me to such suffering when all I wanted to do was love Him and my family.

A year passed, and my parents sent us money for airfare to meet them during the summer at Uncle Aslam's in America. My parents invited Tahir, as they wanted it to be a family vacation, and they didn't want him to feel left out. Tahir was ecstatic, and he was ready to go back to America. When I finally saw my parents, I found the first opportunity to talk to them in private and told them I couldn't stay with Tahir any longer. I explained how terrible things were and I begged them to allow me to leave him. They couldn't believe things were truly as bad as I said, since Tahir put on a great act of love in front of them, and they thought I needed to be mature and not have unreasonable expectations.

"Besides," my mother told me, "life is all about sacrifice and marriage is forever especially if you have a child. What will you do with a child? Finding a man who would accept you with a child and marry you would be nearly impossible, so it was better to adjust with the situation. Life is very difficult."

I wasn't confident enough to fight back, and I had been called emotional and immature by Tahir, and his parents. Now my parents were saying the same thing, so I started to believe it was me who was unreasonable. Without their support, I couldn't leave, as I had no way of supporting my daughter and me. I was at Tahir's mercy. Tahir knew how our culture made it nearly impossible for me to leave him, and he was secure in that knowledge. After two months of vacation and reprieve, I returned to Karachi again, feeling forsaken, barely able to keep up with the steps to the crazy dance of my life.

I wanted the music to stop, the torturous dance to end, so I could catch my breath. I yearned for gentle music to soothe me as I rested in the arms of my lover, but the crashing music pounded on and I had to keep moving, stumbling in the darkness.

CHAPTER 6

United Arab Emirates

Sania turned two years old, and was a bundle of energy with a strong mind of her own. Her beautiful brown hair was always a tangled mess as she barely had the patience to let me tie it, too excited to explore and play. The burden of life got heavier as I watched her, wondering what was going to be her future. I remembered the horrible experience my sisters and I had at the school in Karachi, and I couldn't bear the thought of my daughter going through the same thing. A cold vise-like grip was upon my heart, and I felt that my misery had doubled as now I also mourned for my sweet, innocent daughter.

I was treated more like a nanny than a mother, as my in-laws controlled how my daughter should be raised and totally ignored my wishes. Sania was beginning to view them as the authority figure, and she wouldn't listen to me at all. Tahir was very happy about his parents taking on the role of parenting for Sania, as it made his life easier and less burdensome. The relationship between my in-laws and me became strained, and my father-in-law became ruder and even more insulting. To add to my frustration, he would take off with Sania in the car, sitting in the front seat, without a seatbelt! He was a reckless driver, and when I would find out he took her, I started praying desperately as I waited for her to return. Tahir became totally removed as a parent from these problems and had no thoughts about Sania's future. When I would bring it up, he would get irritated, and we argued.

I tried to discuss schools with Tahir, and his response was, "I don't know what your problem is. There are plenty of schools here, and she will go just as other kids do!"

"But she will have no life here; the education system is so terrible, and we can't even afford to send her to the better school. You and I know the importance of a good education, and what a difference it made for us! How can we not try to give our daughter the same opportunity and instead subject her to a life that will snuff out her identity and joy?"

"She will get used to it! You are emotional and create problems; she will live here like other kids do!"

"Please," I would beg him, "please, at least apply to jobs abroad, you're not happy either," knowing that I was appealing to his selfishness. I knew he was getting bored with the monotony of his job and the life in Karachi, and I knew that if I stroked his ego he might consider the option since he cared about himself much more than his daughter or me!

It worked! He started to look, and soon had an offer from a company in the United Arab Emirates. He decided to take it, and I couldn't believe the news! I was finally going to get out from under his parents and leave Pakistan! There was a glimmer of hope. Allah heard my prayers!

When Tahir told his parents, they were furious. Tahir was their only son, and they expected him to live with and take care of them. They refused to talk to me since they knew I was responsible for pushing Tahir into leaving, and cursed me, saying that I would suffer for what I was doing to them. Like the coward that he was, Tahir blamed me for it and acted like he was helpless because I made his life miserable living in Pakistan. His mother cried and begged him to stay, and in desperation, they even had a family intervention and told him he was committing a sin by abandoning his elderly parents.

They tried everything, but Tahir was now excited about going to a new country and having a change in his life. Travel was his weakness as he had a restless spirit, so staying in one place for long was difficult for him. Now with this opportunity before him, he was willing to overlook his parents' pain and disappointment. For once I was thankful for his selfishness, as that allowed Sania and me to escape from the cruel and constricting life, and I happily took the blame for it.

The United Arab Emirates is a country in the Middle East and is known for its appealing blend of the East and the West. Though it is a Muslim country, women can dress in Western clothes without the requirement to wear a hijab and they can even drive and work if they have permission from their husband or father. There was also no requirement for a woman to be accompanied by a male everywhere as was the case in Saudi Arabia. It allowed me much more freedom than in Pakistan. Though I couldn't drive, I could easily take a cab if I needed to go anywhere, and I could walk to places since it was much safer than Karachi, where looting, kidnapping, and rape were on the rise. The biggest sigh of relief was that my in-laws were not there. What a huge improvement from life in Pakistan, and I soaked it in and thanked Allah for His mercy.

It was not long after we moved there that the first Gulf War began, and there was a serious threat of attack on the UAE. People started to send their families back home, and I panicked at the thought of having to return to Pakistan. I was glued to the news every day, praying for America to stop Saddam Hussein from advancing. CNN reporter Christiane Amanpour, became the most important person in my life as I waited breathlessly for new developments while my life hung on a thread. I would watch with three-year-old Sania playing in our small apartment, desperately praying that Allah would have mercy and not send us back to Pakistan. There were people from Kuwait streaming into the UAE sharing horrifying accounts of their escape, leaving everything they owned behind.

Soon Tahir's company told their employees they should consider sending their families home. When Tahir suggested I return to Karachi with our daughter until things became stable, my heart sank. I told him I wasn't going back; I would live with the outcome. I would rather die than go back to the miserable life in Karachi! Living in a war zone was preferable to the prison of my in-laws' house in Pakistan! Thankfully the situation didn't get worse as the United States finally sent troops to stop Saddam Hussein, and the first Gulf War ended.

A few years went by, and I kept myself busy with my daughter and made new friends. My relationship with my husband continued to be difficult, and we never seemed to agree on anything. I desired a marriage where Tahir and I could be friends, trust each other, and work towards the same common goal of creating a happy home while providing a secure, safe future for our children. Unfortunately, he would not discuss present or future goals, and we were living two separate lives. Without goals and an unknown future, life seemed aimless to me.

The only thing Tahir did want to discuss was how I was negatively affecting his health due to the arguments and all the stress that it caused him. Everything was my fault and my responsibility including the altercations. I felt rejected and alone, and I had to fight to keep my self-esteem. My friends were a thankful distraction, though I never shared my pain with them, as I always tried to keep a respectable front.

We lived in the UAE for ten years, visiting Pakistan every few months. Sadly, I encountered the same lustful advances of Arab men and God protected me from situations that could have led to rape. I was also aware again of a subtle but strong presence of homosexuality, and I realized that the hypocrisy that I had found in Pakistan existed here as well.

A few years after moving to the UAE, my son Hamza was born, and I was hopeful that a second child might awaken a sense of responsibility in Tahir and maybe even love for me. Though Tahir was happy to have a son, he remained indifferent to me and didn't change his attitude towards the family.

Time went quickly for me as I was busy caring for my children. Three times a year we would visit Karachi to keep my in-laws happy and thankfully they were short trips as our relationship was cordial but strained. We also continued to meet my parents once a year at Aunt Naseem and Uncle Aslam's home in the United States. Every year without fail, I would beg my parents to let me stay. My father preferred to keep out of the discussions, and my mother did all the marriage "counseling." She would attempt to reason with my husband that he should be patient, kind, and understanding with me, since I was young. Marriage was about compromise she would tell both of us; we needed to put time and effort into getting along.

My mother failed to realize that my husband did not believe in the kind of marriage that she shared with my father. What they had was built on love, respect, and sacrifice. The building blocks of a successful marriage were missing from my marriage. My mother tried to help us work on relationship issues, because divorce was never an option. Tahir expertly portrayed great patience, and appeared to be a devoted husband and son-in-law who was bearing patiently with their immature and emotional daughter. Every year, the situation escalated. Yet without the physical scars and bruises to prove the abuse and suffering, and considering the psychological and mental strain was invisible, it was difficult for my parents to believe me. They thought I was being childish.

So, at the end of our vacation I would return home with my husband, convinced that I needed to change, grow up, sacrifice, and disregard any feelings, desire, or opinions as they were unrealistic. My marriage continued to deteriorate, and Tahir got colder and more impatient with me with each passing year. My self-esteem continued in a downward spiral, and I lived in fear of making Tahir angry. He used psychological manipulation to keep me insecure and scared to make sure I would never have enough self-worth to leave him. Knowing that my parents would not support my leaving him added to his confidence, and he believed he had me trapped. Truthfully, this worked to his advantage for many years. Although I was in my twenties, I believed I was old, unattractive, and undesirable, and Tahir never missed an opportunity to reinforce that. I began to believe everything he told me, and even began to dislike myself, and I eventually even started to question my sanity. Raising children in this turmoil was a difficult task, but at the same time, Sania and Hamza gave me the purpose and strength to wake up each day.

Tahir soon started traveling for business regularly and was hardly home. Eventually, I realized that he purposely took a traveling position to experience the freedom to live a separate life from his family. The arguments became more frequent between us, and the children began to show signs of fear and confusion as they witnessed the disagreements that had become impossible to hide. Tahir started to openly flirt with my friends and other women in my presence and enjoyed watching my humiliation and pain.

He was taking on more and more of the characteristics of his father, and I felt nauseated, thinking that I would have to bear this for the rest of my life. To add to my pain, I watched his lack of care and concern for the children. My son had severe asthma, and many times needed to be rushed to the hospital in the middle of the night. Since I couldn't drive, I had to take him in a cab, dragging my daughter who was half-asleep, along. I was alone and would panic over my son's precarious health. Sometimes I would call my friend, who was kind enough to come in the middle of the night with her husband and take us to the hospital. All this caused a delay in getting my son to the hospital for treatment, and I feared one day this situation would cost him his life. As I suffered through this ordeal time and time again, I would become furious at Tahir's selfishness and his lack of love for his children. His love for traveling and freedom took precedence over his family, and he was not willing to sacrifice his desires. I had sacrificed myself for years, but now watching his lack of care towards our children filled me with anger.

I started to look forward to him leaving as I couldn't bear being around him. I was more concerned about the children's future because I knew that we could stay in the UAE only as long as he had a job. What would happen if he lost his job? I asked him this question, hoping this time he would have a plan and had considered his children's future, especially as he had received the best education and an opportunity to live outside of Pakistan. His answer was a careless and selfish, "We will move back to Pakistan."

He watched the look of fear and horror on my face with joy then smiled and walked away. That day was the last straw for me. I was constantly sick due to depression, anxiety, and I had even started having suicidal thoughts, but that day I decided I was going to fight for my children! I wanted Sania to have respect and dignity as a woman and a chance at a good education, and I was not going to have my son grow up to be a man like his father and grandfather!

Tahir left to go out of town again, and I called my parents, more determined than ever to leave him. This time my parents heard the resolution in my voice and the truth that I would not survive if I stayed any longer in this toxic situation. They said I could stay with them, but now my parents were living in Pakistan, and I had no desire to go there knowing we would have no future. I knew the Muslim culture would favor my husband and that my children could be taken from me, and I would be forced to return to Tahir.

My sisters lived in Canada, and I could have gone there, but somehow, I knew clearly in my heart that I had to go to America where I believed I would find freedom and protection. I remembered my time in high school and how unhappy I had been there, but now not only was I was ready for that freedom, but I needed it to survive. America was like a city shining on a hill, and I set my sight upon it and called Aunty Naseem.

When she heard how bad things were, she generously offered their home as a refuge until I figured out the next step. I talked to Uncle Aslam who was confident that he could help me find a job through his connections; I could then provide for my children and me. Now that I had a plan in place to leave, my misery turned to hope and a chance for a life not only for myself, but my children. I became filled with courage and strength.

My parents took the situation seriously for the first time and said they would send me money to purchase the tickets for the kids and me, as I knew Tahir would never give me the money. My plan was to tell Tahir that I needed a vacation alone, and I was going to visit Uncle and Aunty in Indiana for the summer. I casually mentioned to him that since he was traveling so much for work, I was going to take the children with me. As I expected, he paid little attention as I was not asking for money from him, and he was busy planning his next trip.

I planned my escape for two months, planning every last detail so my husband would not be suspicious that I had no intention of returning. I feared that if he had any idea, he would stop me from leaving the UAE since the Islamic law favored the man, and my visa was also attached to him. I was his possession, and I had no rights as a woman or mother. I planned to leave on the same day that he returned from a business trip, hoping he would not pay attention to my nervousness or the five large suitcases sitting by the door.

I told the kids we were going on a summer break, not wanting to upset them. Unfortunately, Tahir noticed something was amiss, and this was not an innocent vacation and a few hours before the flight, he hid our passports and refused to take us to the airport, telling me I couldn't leave. Panicking, I begged him for our passports, and he started screaming that he wouldn't allow it. The kids started crying, begging us not to fight. Not knowing what to do, I called my father, crying. For the first time, he showed anger towards Tahir. He told him that he had to let me go as I wasn't well, and Tahir was taken aback by his sternness. Surprisingly, he handed me the passports and seemed to crumble before my eyes. Now that I had the passports, I found the strength to call a cab. Tahir started screaming and then began crying hysterically, begging me to stay.

This tactic of his to my dismay, was one he would use going forward to emotionally manipulate the children and me, since his coldness and anger had lost its hold. Sadly, the children witnessed this display of bogus affection, and by now they were both crying and begging me to stay, which was weakening my resolve. I knew to weaken would be a mistake, and I had to be strong, most of all for their future. My nerves were frayed, and I was shaking with fear by the time we arrived at the airport. I knew Tahir could make one phone call that I was leaving against his wishes with his children, and I could be detained at the airport.

By the time I boarded the plane, I felt like I was having a breakdown. I sat frozen, clutching my children's hands on either side, not wanting to draw attention to myself. I still could be removed from the plane. The kids sat crying silently having witnessed their father's hysterical behavior and traumatized by the chaotic way we left. My heart was breaking for them because I knew they were torn, seeing their father's tears. How could I make them understand this was the best option for the three of us, and the only alternative to maintain my sanity and pave a better future for them?

When the plane finally took off I collapsed in relief. I couldn't believe I made it this far, but until I landed in America, I would not believe I had truly escaped. I promised myself on the flight that my children would never face a situation like mine. I would allow them every opportunity to live in freedom. My fervent hope and prayer was on my mind as I finally dozed off, flying over many seas towards the new country.

I had torn myself away from the crashing music that was destroying me, but now my heart pounded in fear and anticipation about the new, unknown dance. Would my children and I be able to learn a new dance to a foreign rhythm?

PART 2

AWAKENING

"In the dark night of the soul, bright flows the river of God."

– *St. John of the Cross*

NIKKI KINGSLEY

CHAPTER 7

Last Cry of Darkness

We landed in the United States in July of 1999, exhausted and in a daze. My aunt and uncle picked us up from the airport, and I remember looking out of the car window and breathing in freedom and peace for the first time in many years. The music was starting to change, setting the stage to lead me to a new dance, but the music that had accompanied me for the last thirteen years had affected me deeply. I was numb to the change and glad the punishing beat had ended.

I was besieged by guilt over the next few weeks as I watched my children's sadness and their constant questions about their father. My children's last memory was of him crying, and being too young to realize the rejection they had been subject to over the years, they continued to mourn for him. I felt deep sorrow and guilt for my children's anguish for taking them away from their father, and to a completely different world. I knew they were confused and hurt. I was grateful my sister Zara came to spend several weeks with us, offering support through this transition that was so painful and difficult.

My sisters and I had drifted apart, only because of distance and my sad situation that left me without energy for much else. But our love for each other never waned, and now that I was close, Zara came to stand by me. This began a closer and deeper relationship with my sisters as they supported me wholeheartedly in my decision to leave Tahir. They were both married now and able to understand my situation. Maji was thankfully living with my aunt and uncle, and her calming and loving presence was not only a balm to my broken heart, but she was a loving strength to my children as well. I struggled to transition to the new country, culture, and life situation. Slowly I picked myself up, realizing I had much work to do if we were to stay in this new country and begin a new life.

First on the list was learning to drive, and Uncle Aslam instructed me in his expensive Lexus! He said I had nothing to fear, explaining I could do or be anything I desired, as long as I was prepared to work hard. I went on job interviews, opened a bank account, and enrolled my children in school for the fall. As I experienced these freedoms, the contrast to my previous life became even starker. I grieved over the years spent in bondage under the manipulation and control of an insecure, sadistic husband and his family and the oppressive culture that used fear and dependency to wield power. In contrast, this was the direct opposite of the world I left behind, and I thanked God for the United States of America, a country that was for me a beacon of light that offered equality and freedom.

Uncle Aslam shared my sentiments saying, "America is the greatest country in the world. I have traveled and lived in Asia, Europe, and Africa, but America is the only place that permits every person an equal opportunity to be successful and build a good life." My uncle was a patient and kind man, taking time from his busy work schedule to teach me basic lessons in living independently.

My parents sent money to help me, and I went with Uncle Aslam to buy my first car. I was thirty years old when I walked through the used car lot with him and picked out a black Toyota Rav4. I drove alone for the first time following him home, and the freedom I felt was incredible, feeling exhilarated and scared at the same time. I couldn't believe that I could go somewhere on my own without being dependent on someone else. I was also acutely aware that with freedom came responsibility. Now I would be responsible for the consequences of my actions because for the first time, these were my choices.

Aunty Naseem and my mother, who by now had come to America to deal with my situation, greeted us in the driveway, their faces showing shock and disapproval. They were not happy that Uncle Aslam had brought me to buy a car so quickly. To them, it seemed like he was giving me too much freedom, and though they loved me, it seemed subconsciously they too struggled with allowing me freedom. Uncle Aslam told them that it was a basic first step and necessary if I was to begin a life in America and get a job. The money my father sent was to help me with living expenses. However I decided to buy a car and this signaled more independence than my parents were comfortable with me having at this time. In addition, my mother was secretly hoping that I would eventually reconcile with Tahir. Now after this freedom, she feared I would not return to him, and she was right.

My mother was blessed to have a wonderful marriage, and she was unable to comprehend that mine could be any different, especially if I didn't have the physical scars to prove the abuse. Maji sided with me. She knew and understood me well from all the years we spent together, and she continued to tell my mother that it was not healthy to force me to stay with Tahir.

"It is irrelevant that Tahir is good to us if he is not good to Naylah. All that matters is how it is for her, and we have to support her." At around eighty-eight years of age, Maji had a wisdom and strength that was not enslaved to the culture or religion that gave women no importance.

The three months I lived with Aunty Naseem and Uncle Aslam were emotionally exhausting as my mother worked hard to encourage

61

me to change my mind about divorcing Tahir, fearful of the family and culture that would reject my children and me as outcasts.

A divorce leaves a stain on the woman and the children in Islam, whereas it has no effect on the man. My mother's greatest worry was how society would treat us and no one would want to marry me with two children. Though she knew every embarrassing detail of my unhappy marriage, this fear was greater for her than my suffering. Sania and Hamza were eleven and seven now, and they were upset and confused with the discussions. They knew life had changed for us forever, and they sensed the sadness and fear that surrounded me. Overhearing the arguments with my mother didn't help, as I desperately tried to explain to her how I could not possibly live with their father. I was constantly plagued by self-doubt, as my mother continued to question my decision and as I watched my children's pain. The burden of guilt was a heavy one to carry.

To add to the confusion, Tahir showed up crying and begging for me to return, putting on a great display of love. He had been embarrassed by my leaving him, and he needed me back to maintain the façade of a happy family. I was having an emotional breakdown, as I tried to justify my decision, to explain it in a way that my family would understand, and I sought compassion and support from my mother. I was glad she didn't invite him to stay with us at Uncle Aslam's as that would have been too much for me to bear. To add to my burden, though Uncle Aslam seemed to be as kind as ever, I knew that I had overstayed my welcome in the two months, and I had to move out soon.

Thankfully Zara came to visit again and having her by my side gave me strength through the struggle and the courage to stand my ground as she and Maira wanted me to be healthy and happy and did not care about the Muslim culture or what people would think. They tried their best, like Maji, to help my mother overcome her fear, but to no avail. My father was more supportive of my decisions, but since he was still in Pakistan, he didn't have much influence on my mother's opinions. Thankfully Tahir had to go back to the UAE to his job, and my mother returned to Pakistan shortly after that. I was finally relieved from the emotional pressure, and using the rest of the money from my father, I took the next big step and moved into my first apartment with my children. Thankfully Maji came with me to help me adjust to living on my own for the first time. I breathed a sigh of relief as I didn't want to impose any longer on my uncle and aunt, and things were quiet for the first time, allowing me to spend time with the children in peace.

The next biggest obstacle to my freedom was finding a job, and thankfully Uncle Aslam's contacts came through. I was able to get a job that paid enough to allow me to support the three of us. The job was in marketing and sales, and that gave me the flexibility to pick up and drop off my children who had just started school. It was ideal for my situation, but completely incompatible with my shy and introverted personality. To me, books were more appealing than human company, but this marketing position required me to spend my day interacting with people and developing business relationships.

I was grateful for the opportunity and needed the income, so I quickly learned as much as possible. I wanted to understand the business and make sure I excelled. The first few months were very difficult with the children beginning school in a foreign country and culture. I was adjusting to my new life where I was responsible for bills, the home, the children, and the new job. Though the job was challenging and not suited for my personality, the biggest relief was that there was no one criticizing me, or trying to psychologically destroy me or my self-image.

While I understood the business and I spoke English fluently, I found as I interacted with clients that I didn't understand the nuances of what they were saying, even though we were speaking the same language. The references they made, the jokes, discussion about sports and other topics people typically talked about were foreign to me. I became stressed each morning at the thought of making small talk, and building relationships seemed impossible. After all, what did I have in common with these people who had lived such a different life than me? I reminded myself that I couldn't afford to fail because that would mean defeat and a return to Tahir, something I couldn't imagine ever doing. Every day, after a few business calls, I would sit in the car and cry, feeling I couldn't go to one more client. I felt emotionally drained because of the struggle to connect with the clients, the pressure from my mother to reconcile with Tahir, and the fear of being forced back to Pakistan if I lost my job since my visa was attached to my job.

Uncle Aslam continued to help by introducing me to his contacts that supported me with business, which helped me to meet my sales goals. Things started to change after a few painful months at work, and I slowly opened up and started to share my situation and develop friendships with the clients. The women affirmed me and my decision, including the right to my dignity as a human being. It was the first time anyone told me with strong conviction and clear terms that I deserved better, and that my life had value, meaning, and purpose. I didn't only have to be only a daughter, wife, or mother. As these wonderful women were encouraging me, my culture was doing the opposite.

The male clients with Middle Eastern origin looked at me like spoiled goods. Their actions and words suggested I had no worth since I was going through a divorce, and I should be happy and grateful for their attention. Most were married, obviously open to having an affair, and happy to tell me this was very normal. After all, I would be the lucky one to have their attention. Who else could want me now? I kept a distance from them and made sure I wasn't ever alone with them. I walked a fine line as I couldn't afford to offend them and affect my business.

I had started going to the Ismaili mosque with my family, and it gave my children and me a place to belong. Some of the wives kept a close eye on me in case I planned on luring their husbands. I was aware of the piercing eyes following me, watching their husbands closely. Besides this, most of the people at the mosque were friendly, and I was able to make a few friends who helped me feel settled. I was also happy to see the children were beginning to form friendships and become involved in activities.

Though the social aspect of the faith was great, the Ismaili faith still failed to touch my heart. So, I continued to practice the Sunni faith at home, saying the *namaz* and reading the Quran which made me feel like I was loyal to Allah and Mohammad. I would go to the Ismaili mosque on Fridays for social purposes but would say the *namaz* at home every day, continuing to beg Allah to help me out of this darkness.

My movements were still uncertain as I listened closely and watched, trying to learn the beat and join the beautiful and confident dancers in this new city, as they twirled away freely and confidently. But it wasn't time yet; I had one more dance left to finish in the darkness.

My parents came sometime later to visit, still very concerned about me living on my own, and I could feel their sadness and worry. It seemed the decision to leave my husband to save my life had disrupted the lives of people I loved the most. My self-esteem was wounded, and I believed that my life wasn't worth anything, because I was taught that my primary concern should be to please and serve others and disregard my own feelings. Pressure to reconcile with Tahir began directly and indirectly, and this only fueled my negative thoughts about myself. I watched my children's pain and confusion over the separation from their father, as well as my parents' fear and disappointment over the failed marriage and the disgrace on the family. I felt extremely guilty and responsible for causing so much pain and having no space to assess my pain.

I longed for someone to ask how I was feeling—me as a person, not as a mother, daughter, or wife, titles that had been thrust on me too early in life. I desperately needed encouragement and affirmation, and that never came, and instead I felt selfish for thinking about myself as I watched the pain of my children and parents. The burden eventually became too heavy to carry, and the guilt of being the cause of suffering broke me, and I finally gave up. I was tired of the mental anguish and guilt, which never seemed to cease though I had escaped from Tahir. I reluctantly agreed to reconcile with Tahir, who had by now called my whole extended family, crying and begging for them to convince me to change my mind. Strangely enough, he seemed to have wilted since I left, and felt no shame in crying to everyone.

He had lost his job in the UAE, and my father advised me in private that I should not leave my job, but let Tahir move in with me. This would ensure that I would have my independence in case it did not work out. I was surprised that he was leaving that door open. I agreed since I would never go back to the prison that I had escaped from. My husband moved in, and I instantly felt like a lead weight came upon my heart, and it seemed that all my struggling had been for nothing. Everything that I had worked so hard to escape had failed. I had lost! I was back in this unhealthy relationship, but by now I couldn't even bear to be in the same room as him. My skin would crawl when he came near me, and I had to tolerate it all and smile for the children's sake, who were watching very closely. In their innocence, they wanted us together, unable to see the darker side of their father.

Once again, I felt depressed, but this time I could barely get up to go to work. It was so bad that I was prescribed medication to help with depression and anxiety, which only gave me a false and superficial sense of wellness, as my heart continued to be heavy. Through the difficulties and challenges I faced in the last year in starting a new life in America, I never felt the despair that I felt now. In the struggle to make a new life there had been hope, but now all I felt was darkness and hopelessness and a feeling of failure to escape.

It was obvious that I had no feelings for Tahir, and that he had no desire to change anything about himself for the family. Instead, he had an underlying anger against me which was palpable because I had shamed and disrespected him in the family and society by leaving him. Although he made claims of undying love for me, I knew that he hated me. It was clear to me that I was healthier without him than with him, and I knew without a doubt that this would never work. It was unfair to both of us to force this façade of a marriage and endure the daily arguing which was inescapable because we agreed on nothing, and it certainly wasn't a healthy environment for the children.

Through this tumultuous time, my relationship with God stayed consistent. Thankfully I didn't blame Him for my suffering that would have been very easy, as I would constantly hear from my mother that this suffering was my *kismet* (destiny), meaning preordained by God!

I was more confused than angry with God. I didn't understand why my life had been snatched away from me. There were other women in my culture, even in my own family, that had more freedom and a wonderful life, while I had never had a chance. Why had I been handed over to a man as property? Why was I never allowed to mature and learn what marriage was and to develop myself as a person? I wondered if I had offended Allah and this was the punishment.

I prayed a lot, still believing that He would help me and had something better in store for me if I trusted Him. God had given me the gift of hope even though my situation was dark, according to all of the dire predictions from my culture, which believed life was only going to get worse since I was a divorced woman with two children. The only hope for me was that I might get lucky and catch the eye of an older widowed man who was kind hearted enough to accept me with my baggage.

I refused to believe that was my only option, and I begged Allah to help me; I told Him I trusted Him and that I knew He had a better plan for me and prostrated myself every day before him. Though I couldn't feel Him at all, I strongly believed that He was all powerful and would take care of my children and me because He loved me. How I believed this I cannot explain as in the Muslim religion we are not taught about God's love and saving power, but more about the fear; whereas in the Ismaili mosque, education and success was the main topic and basis of the preaching. Now that Tahir was back in our lives, it was difficult for us to go to the Ismaili mosque as he was Sunni and couldn't participate, and so our newly-established routine which was helping us establish roots was changed again.

My parents meanwhile were relieved when Tahir and I reconciled, and they left soon afterward, hoping that the separation and new environment would help our relationship. They settled in Canada, living close to Maira and Zara who were married, but thankfully had been spared the ordeal of an arranged marriage. My parents still did not seem to grasp the fact that Tahir and I were incompatible as our desires and priorities didn't match. The environment couldn't change such fundamental flaws. They held on to hope that Tahir and I could make it work out and save the family from fracturing, especially for the sake of Sania and Hamza.

A few months later, Tahir found a job, and soon to his delight, was traveling once again. He became restless and bored if he didn't have an upcoming trip, and it was obvious he did not desire to live a normal routine life with his family, and he had arranged his career path in a way that ensured he constantly traveled. This suited me well now as the separation gave me the space to think and decide on my next move. Things were not any better as I saw nothing had changed with him. He wasn't a man who had come close to losing his family and now was treasuring his wife and children; in fact, he was back to doing what he wanted.

Since I was now earning money, he felt even less responsible. He joked one day that since I was working, he didn't mind letting me provide. That was the last straw for me. He was a terrible husband, an irresponsible and disconnected father, and now he wanted me to support him! It seemed that this man had no pride, and I couldn't find anything in him that I could respect, something that I believed was necessary even before love. There was no reason left for me to stay in this marriage and suffer, especially since I wasn't a prisoner anymore.

I called Uncle Aslam and met with him, explaining that the reconciliation was not working out and I couldn't do it anymore, and to my surprise, he told me that I had made my choice and now I had to live with the decision I had made. I knew this time I was not going to get any support, as he too seemed tired of the situation and did not want to deal with the problems this would once again cause the family. This time I was convinced beyond a shadow of a doubt that I had to leave Tahir. I was not going to spend the rest of my life medicated to tolerate living with someone I didn't love and who didn't love me or care about our family.

I filed for divorce, and felt much stronger this time around, as I had no doubt about my decision and would have no regrets in the future. In the end, I wish I could say that Tahir and I both made a mature and mutual decision to end the marriage, but it wasn't so. We went through a long and painful divorce that ended fifteen years of marriage, and it left behind a lot of anger and resentment that would take many years to heal.

I could tell the music had finally changed. The painful throbbing sound was silenced, and a new melody was beginning. The gentle and velvety notes were foreign to me. They touched my ears softly, as if aware of the damage caused by the pounding music, and slowly I started to sway with the music letting the notes softly caress me.

CHAPTER 8

A Cultural Transition

I remained vulnerable from the bitter divorce, but tried to adjust to my life working and living as a single parent. Quite unexpectedly, Simon entered my life during a crazy morning at work. It was Monday morning, and after the rush of driving my children to school, I was rear-ended on the way to work. Emotionally, I was worn out as I was fighting the guilt and anxiety of the big step I had just taken with the divorce. I ran, frazzled and exhausted, into a meeting. Standing with his arms crossed was a dark-haired man, waiting with my manager and the rest of the staff. As the meeting began, I listened as the manager introduced this new person, Simon, who was going to be our new area manager.

My heart sank as I knew I had not made a good first impression! What if this new boss fired me? I would have to leave the country! My whole life was hanging on this job, and in the hands of this stranger who looked stern and not very pleased with my late entrance.

As Simon spoke, I forced the fear out of my mind and tried to pay attention through the meeting. After a few weeks, I realized I was not going to lose my job, which was my biggest fear. I learned quickly that Simon was not as serious or stern as I first thought. In fact he was rarely serious, and displayed a great sense of humor. It was obvious he was very good at his job, and soon we all looked forward to his visits at our branch. He lightened the mood with his jokes and sense of humor, which very unusual for me, as no man had made me laugh. The last time I remembered laughing was with my cousin Amber, and that had been nearly twenty years ago!

Simon and I became friends. It happened so quickly that I didn't notice. Our friendship was gradual, and many times at work I would catch myself laughing and would be shocked that it was a man from a different culture who was making me laugh. Simon would make sure I was not left alone for lunch or dinner during meetings, and when he noticed I didn't understand many of nuances that were part of the conversation, he would explain things and make me feel included. Simon reminded me of my best friend Ahsan from Dar.

As our friendship grew, I soon noticed how I arranged my schedule to make sure I would be in the office when he came. I knew that my feelings had grown to more than just being friends, and I felt nervous about what that meant. I had never dated, and this was a man from a Western culture. I didn't know if I was reading too much into the friendship, but I was pretty sure he thought of me as more than a friend.

This kindness and attention Simon showed me started to heal my wounded self-esteem. He also never made me feel uncomfortable. Slowly, he started to ask me questions about how I felt about things and what I liked or didn't like. I realized that I didn't know the answers. No one had cared enough to ask me my opinions or thoughts. I had begged and cried for that, and had been ignored as immature, emotional, and finally tolerated. But this man seemed genuinely interested in me. Strangely, I found that I had no idea how I did feel! I would get frustrated with his questions when I didn't know the answers nor want to embarrass myself. I would change the subject, and Simon gently kept asking until I started to think about what I did and didn't like. He was slowly helping me to discover who I was.

My life started to be filled with happiness that I had never had. I realized that I didn't have a need for the medication that I had been taking to help me through each day. I enjoyed the special attention from this American man. What was I going to do? In my wildest dreams, I had never envisioned myself marrying anyone outside of my culture and religion. I had so much trouble understanding the nuances of the American culture, and the move had been so difficult along with the process of adjusting, I never considered a relationship. After all, what would we have in common? In fact, I used to think that people who married out of their culture and religion were making a big mistake; they could never make their relationship work with all the differences.

What amazed me the most about Simon was that he genuinely seemed interested in me. I found that I was easily sharing my past, my struggles, and fears without being judged. I couldn't understand how I was so comfortable with a complete foreigner from a different culture. The differences that had seemed so huge to me at one time seemed to fade away– thanks to Simon's easygoing nature.

He showed interest in understanding my culture, religion, language, and also loved the food. Though I had traveled a lot, I was kept from many things. In my culture, we were not encouraged to try anything new. I watched Simon closely when he met my children at several employee family events as my feelings would have changed if he were distant or unkind. I was very protective of Sania and Hamza after what they had suffered. I saw Simon's kindness, and soon that fear was laid to rest.

One day Simon casually suggested that we see a movie, and I tried to act normal and agreed, offering to meet him there as I didn't want the kids or Maji to see me going out with a man. That was our first "date." It felt like we were the best of friends, and I felt completely safe and comfortable with him. We met out a few times after that, and it was obvious that Simon cared about me. I knew he would never approach me. He was in the same dilemma about my culture; he was not sure what would be appropriate. What if I was offended? He feared it would end our friendship. Months went by and finally one Friday after work, standing by my car reluctantly saying goodbye, I suddenly blurted out, "Do you think about me as much as I think about you?"

We both looked at each other shocked– me at what had slipped out, and him– incredulous at what he heard. I felt my face burn with embarrassment and I mumbled "Goodbye" and jumped in my car and drove off. I couldn't believe what I said. How shameful for a woman to be so forward, I thought. How could I ever face Simon again? As soon as I started driving, the phone rang, and it was Simon. I could barely say hello– my mouth dry and my face still on fire.

"I think about you as much, if not more, when we are not together. I was too scared of offending you as I know things are different in your culture."

I couldn't believe what I was hearing as my heart was doing somersaults. Was I living a romance out of one of my books and was it finally happening to me? Simon said he planned on pursuing a relationship with me with the intention of marriage since he knew I would not date casually. We talked openly about our feelings now and enjoyed this new stage of our relationship for a few more weeks. I was amazed that I had no doubts at all, even though we had known each other for only a short time.

With the discussion of marriage came the discussion of faith, because during this time I was practicing Islam faithfully, and according to Islam a woman could not marry a non-Muslim as that would be adultery. I had barely found peace with my divorce in Allah's eyes, and I did not want to start off this new life by offending Him. I wanted to do everything right so Allah would bless the marriage. Simon, at that time, was a non-practicing Catholic, but a believer of Christianity not attending any particular church. I was totally ignorant about the sects of Christianity, though I had some exposure through my earlier year in Indiana. I was so convinced about Islam being the only truth that I didn't care to know about any other faith.

I shared my desire to get married in the mosque, and for that to happen, Simon was willing to say one sentence (*Shahdah*) that would make him Muslim, and keep my relationship right with Allah. I told Simon that God was very important to me. Simon looked at it simply, and if it gave me peace of mind, and kept my relationship right with Allah, then he would convert to Islam. I also realized my children suffered many changes and this sacrifice from him would unify the family, and foster stability. I realized most of the people I knew at the Ismaili mosque would not care about whether we were married in the mosque or not; they were pretty liberal. However, this was something I wanted to do for my love of Allah and desire to please Him.

My parents came to visit, and I told them about my decision to marry Simon. They were shocked and upset, pointing out that the chances of this marriage being successful was slim due to all the differences of culture and religion, which would also be difficult for the children. I explained our relationship and love as best as I could, along with his consent for my sake to get married in the mosque. They agreed to meet him and I was sure that they would approve– and they did.

Simon did not have any children of his own, but had a desire to help my children to make up for what they had lost over the years. Thankfully Sania and Hamza were comfortable and happy around him too. Eventually, when I asked them how they felt if I was to marry him, they were agreeable. Simon and I had a beautiful, traditional Pakistani wedding after the religious ceremony in the mosque. My son was eleven and my daughter was fourteen when we became a family, and I will always be grateful for their love and trust in me that allowed them to bring Simon into their lives.

The next couple of years were spent adjusting and settling into our new family life. We attended the mosque on Fridays so the children would have a sense of continuity and belonging. Twice a week a Sunni Quran teacher came to the home, like all of my other Sunni friends, to make sure they received the Islamic faith and could read Quran in Arabic which was very important for a Muslim. I was trying hard to keep the children grounded in the faith and would force them every evening to pray *namaz* together, teaching my daughter how to cover her head correctly for prayer, and all of the cleansing rituals. The children hated it! They grumbled every day when it was time for prayer, and especially when Sister Amira came to teach Quran and the rules of Islam. They found it meaningless, and they hated the fact that everything was based on fear of Hell. However, I insisted, desperately trying to hold on to the Islamic faith and pass it on to my children.

Tahir, who had visiting rights with our children, tried his best to inflict as much damage as possible and pull both of them toward him— — poisoning their minds against me. He used tears and emotional blackmail to keep their sympathy, and whenever they visited him in England where he was now living, they came back upset and confused. The children's visits with their father were frequent during my first year of marriage to Simon. This was so difficult for me, as I barely got them emotionally healthy again when it was time for them to leave to see their father once more. The same upheaval happened if Tahir came into town to the United States to visit them. His hatred for me was visible and palpable when I would have to face him or talk to him regarding our children.

Thankfully Simon took on the financial responsibility for the children, so their father was not dependent on supporting them. However, Tahir still made life as difficult as possible for me. He continued his negative behavior, which backfired, and only helped in ensuring I suffered no regrets about leaving him!

Simon, in contrast, started to become a father figure to both Sania and Hamza. It turned out that having Simon in this role was a gift for my children as it helped them acclimate into American culture. My children would never have experienced the trips, sports, or push to be independent without Simon's influence since these were things that I had no experience or exposure to myself. Simon seemed always two steps ahead of the three of us.

I swayed to the gentle and sweet melody, a sweet contrast to the painful music of the past. I was being guided through the steps we knew, creating a new dance to a new melody.

CHAPTER 9

Moderate Muslim

As life settled into a peaceful routine for me for the first time, my heart renewed its desire for God. Now I wanted to spend time getting to know Him instead of only turning to Him in pain and crying out for help. The many years of difficult circumstances had strangled my desires, and all I could do was survive, but now as the challenges subsided and life became peaceful, the thirst that had always been in my heart to know the truth about God started to ignite again.

I was praying *namaz* regularly, fasting during Ramadan, the Islamic month of fasting, and reading the Quran every day. Simon would join me to try and understand my faith that was most important to me. I didn't know Arabic so I would read a transliteration and a translation of the Quran. Since now I wasn't just imploring Allah's mercy, I started to reflect on what I was reading. I came across certain verses that disturbed and confused me with their violence and rejection of non-Muslims, but I put it down due to my lack of understanding. After all, Muslims are taught that the proper understanding of the Quran is only possible in Arabic, and any translation falls short of the true meaning. Based on that teaching of the faith, only Arabic-speaking Muslims could understand the true meaning of the Quran, whereas other Muslims could recite the words, but never fully understand.

I was searching for a deeper relationship with Allah and no matter how much I prayed and how perfectly I tried to follow the rules, it seemed to me that I stood before a closed door. All I experienced during prayer was silence and darkness, and I couldn't understand why I was getting no response though I loved Allah with all my heart. None of my many Muslim friends or relatives expressed a similar desire for a relationship or response from Allah. They seemed satisfied in following the rules, rituals, and doing their part faithfully in the hope of making it into Paradise. Once they fulfilled all the requirements, it seemed that they were able to move on to do other things. My mind never fully accepted things as quietly and obediently as most of my Muslim friends.

I had difficulty living on the surface as a Muslim, but never looking beneath the crust that seemed to be full of cracks. I continued to have questions and thoughts about Allah, and an ache in my heart to know Him more fully. I couldn't understand why I was not satisfied like them—there must be something I was missing. I knew that Islam was the only path to Allah, so why wasn't He answering me? I was not satisfied with my prayers alone, as it seemed one sided. I wanted a response from Him, and I believed there was much more on the other side of that door. I knew the Truth was there, and I yearned for it, so I did what I was trained to do and kept prostrating myself before Him, begging Allah to reveal Himself. I shared my frustration and this struggle with Simon, but because I was determined to find the answer within Islam, all he could offer me was an ear.

I believed that there was an objective Truth, not different versions. How could there be many Truths? It didn't make sense as Truth would lose its meaning if there was more than one Truth. I didn't want to create my truth; I wanted to find the Truth. I knew the answer lay behind the wall that I couldn't get past, and I knew that once I found it, I would know God and discover Truth.

Married for two years, I settled into a routine which was work, children, and a social life that consisted mainly of my Muslim friends. Simon adjusted to my culture and was trying hard to keep things harmonious and peaceful for the family. Though I loved America, its freedom and opportunities that it had provided my children and me, I still missed some aspects of my culture. Most of my friends were from Pakistan and were Sunni Muslim. This allowed me to hold on to the things I missed, like the language, food, faith, and other familiar traditions. We were "moderate Muslims," which meant we dressed in Western clothes, spoke in Urdu that was liberally sprinkled with English, and worked and mingled with men. We kept the Muslim rules like not eating pork or drinking alcohol, praying and fasting, and some who were stricter only eating *halaal* meat. (This is similar to kosher, except a Muslim prayer is recited at the slaughtering of the animal.) These friendships gave me a connection to my culture which I wanted to hold on to, but in my heart, I knew that I never truly fit in.

It appeared that my friends found peace with the way they lived their lives, and the comfortable version of Islam they followed. They didn't seem to pursue a relationship with Allah, but rather wanted to follow the precepts of Islam and get into Paradise. They dismissed violence or other difficult-to-stomach verses of the Quran as a flaw in the translation. A Muslim couldn't question or criticize any of the teachings of Islam for fear of sounding like he or she had a weak faith, and to doubt was regarded as a grave sin. When I questioned any teaching that seemed unjust or any violence that was happening in the name of Islam, my friends rejected it with the most common excuses that it was the wrong interpretation. Or, the argument could quickly change and focus on themselves and how they were fearful of being harassed. It bothered me tremendously that there was no acknowledgment and discussion on the violent acts, but rather a focus on themselves and how they might be victimized. I struggled internally since I was very committed to Islam. I asked questions only because I wanted to understand my faith better, so it could grow stronger and deeper. I wanted to have open and balanced discussions and lay my questions to rest. I longed to joyfully follow my faith in full measure. However, no one could answer me in a way that gave me peace.

I kept these thoughts in my heart and continued to push the children towards the Islamic practices, though Sania and Hamza were becoming more and more vocal about how they didn't agree with what Sister Amira was teaching. One day, frustrated after her class, Sania declared that she thought Christianity was a better religion. She said it seemed peaceful and loving, whereas all she heard from Sister Amira was hate and fear. After making this declaration, she angrily threw off her veil and stormed away. In contrast, Hamza, being of a gentle nature, watched my face, fearing I would cry. He had seen me cry so many times, all he wanted was for me to be happy. I kept it together in front of him, but my heart sank!

I had failed to pass the faith to my children and disappointed Allah. I would have to face the shame, and all my friends and family would say that it was because of the divorce and marrying a white man! Thankfully this never came up again from Sania, and I continued to firmly push them to practice the faith, hoping I would eventually find reconciliation with my conflicting thoughts and help them as well.

I believed God gave us a mind to reason and follow the objective good, and it would only glorify Him when we would use it to search for Him, so I couldn't understand why Allah would forbid reason and encourage fear. Undoubtedly there were some teachings of mercy and peace in the Quran and *hadiths* (teachings of the Prophet Mohammad), but there were also many verses on violence that made it ambiguous and confusing. Reading the many teachings of Islam based on the *hadiths*, I found only long lists of rules that were hard to take seriously and were repressive for women. Certain actions of the Prophet Mohammad were equally disturbing.

For example, a Muslim should use only the left hand when washing one's private parts, blowing one's nose, or holding any dirty object. No intoxicants, board games, or games of chance are allowed. And then there were lists of rules for women to follow, for the fear was that men might be sexually aroused if women didn't cover themselves appropriately. Though many Muslims don't follow these rules or are not aware of them, they do still exist. I also couldn't understand why these men who prayed so often and followed such strict rules could be so weak and carnal that they couldn't look at a woman without being aroused and losing control? Why did the full responsibility fall on the women instead of men being instructed to overcome their temptations? These were the same men who acted holy and filled the mosques. I wondered how these men could be devout Muslims and act in such a shameful way. Sadly, this behavior was common and accepted by society, with women being told to dress more modestly. When I brought up some of these questions in conversation with my Muslim friends in the hope of an answer to my conflicting thoughts, as always, all I received were shocked looks and a change of subject. As moderates, we ignored much of the oppressive rules and teachings but that did not change the fact about the faith.

One explanation I often heard in moderate circles was that the Quran is understandable to a learned few who are well versed in Arabic. But then, my mind argued, why would God reveal His law and make it understandable only to a few? Wouldn't that defeat the purpose? Plus, the learned ones, the Muslim scholars who had PhDs in Islamic theology supported the violence and oppression of women, so how could a moderate Muslim, who usually didn't speak Arabic or have a theology degree, deny it? I was not able to reconcile my conscience with the complete teaching of Islam, so I too chose which part I could follow and thus was a moderate Muslim, confused, but wholeheartedly desiring to know Allah.

Meanwhile, my daily prayers continued, and I would show up before God every day and beg Him to speak to me. I wanted to know Him. I longed for Him, and I wanted to feel peace and joy practicing all of Islam. I was uncomfortable with the picture of God that Islam painted in my mind. My vision of God was gentle and kind, embracing all people and showing mercy and kindness and always calling us to Himself. I couldn't accept that Allah would give us a brain to reason but then ask us not to use it but follow him blindly and call his followers to violence. Why was Allah's message so confusing and contradictory? The God in my heart and the Allah of Islam were difficult to reconcile and left me frustrated. So I struggled with this and prayed fervently, as I never doubted Islam itself, but continued to blame my lack of understanding and kept searching for the objective truth that I knew existed.

Now I was finally dancing to gentle music in the arms of my lover, but suddenly the dance floor seemed unstable and filled with shadows, making me uncertain where to move. Trying to keep the rhythm, I rested in my lover's arms, trusting Him to lead me through the shifting shadows on to solid ground.

CHAPTER 10

The Encounter

God who is rich in mercy had been listening to me closely, but was waiting for the perfect time to call me and show His glory. Finally, the time arrived, and God was going to answer my pleas after many years, but my fear and my Muslim faith wasn't going to make it easy. I had created a box for God, and I expected Him to fit into it neatly, but God's ways are not our ways, and so began my tango with God.

In the spring of 2005 we went on a family vacation to New York, and standing in Times Square, I was amazed at the number of people and the hustle and bustle. There was so much to see and do, and Simon being the organizer, had our days planned from morning until night.

One of the places he had on the list was St. Patrick's Cathedral—being a Muslim— I wasn't interested in seeing a church. There were so many other places to see, and the last place I wanted to visit was to a Christian Cathedral! Simon insisted we had to see it. After all, it was recommended as one of the top-rated tourist spots, and he was convinced that the kids and I would regret missing this monumental structure. I reluctantly agreed for his sake, but in my heart, I was feeling guilty since this was a Christian church, and Allah would not be pleased with me for going to a place where statues were worshipped, and Christians believed in a Son of God, which was considered blasphemy!

On a beautiful sunny morning, reminding Allah that I was doing this for my husband, while asking for Allah's forgiveness, I entered St Patrick's Cathedral. It was majestic and seemed to defy the modernization that surrounded it, appearing to make a bold statement that it stood for something that was unchanging throughout time.

As we walked in, I was amazed at the beauty, and immediately a sense of deep peace filled me. Feeling as if I had entered another world, I savored the peace. As I stood inside, looking in awe at the grand beauty, my eyes met another pair of piercing eyes on a stained glass hanging down from the ceiling. It was the face of Jesus, and I was mesmerized. I stared back at Him and felt His eyes burning right through me, looking into my soul. The intensity scared me, and I looked away, trying to ignore it, but no matter where I went, it seemed His eyes were following me, and I couldn't get away. We walked around, admiring the beauty of the Cathedral, though in my heart, I felt fearful that I was offending Allah by participating in the blasphemous belief and idolatry just by being present. While all of these thoughts were nagging me, I couldn't ignore the peace that had settled over me. With these conflicting feelings, I tried to move us along quickly, the fear in my mind rising to squash the peace that was gently touching my heart.

I was finally standing by the exit, looking at the gift table, when I first heard the sweet and tender whisper, "Come back." It was a clear call coming from within me, but I knew it was not me or my mind. As I wondered what was happening, I heard it again, and again. "Come back. Come back."

I immediately understood that it was Mary, (she identified herself as Mary, not Maryam), but I understood her. She was calling me to her chapel that I had passed on the way out. I ignored the voice initially, talking to the children as we looked at the souvenirs, thinking I was imagining the voice, but she was insistent.

Since I knew Mary as a Muslim, and having great love and respect for her, I couldn't ignore the sweet voice that persistently called. I finally relinquished and my family that I would return shortly, and I made my way to the little chapel that had Mary's statue. I stood there thinking she would tell me what she wanted, or why she had called me, but I heard nothing. I witnessed people deep in prayer, kneeling before her statue. Their faith and love was on display without shame, and I saw gentleness and trust that moved my heart. I finally sat down and told Mary that I was here waiting, and asked what she wanted. I waited to hear that gentle voice again, but she was silent. I told her I wasn't going to kneel before her statue, though I loved her, as it was against Islam.

Moved by the love displayed for Mary by the people, it became obvious they had a personal relationship with her, but I felt sorry for them as they didn't know that they were lost and committing a grave sin before Allah as they had bent their knees before an idol. Little did I know then that they weren't worshipping her, but honoring her as Mother of Jesus and asking her intercession before the Throne of God.

As I was reasoning about why this was wrong, my heart was marveling at the love I could feel from the worshippers. I had never witnessed such a personal prayer or display of love in Islam. I had seen Muslims praying the *namaz* in unison many times, going through all the rituals, chanting all the prayers together, which had seemed beautiful, but the depth of worship that I was witnessing here was much more profound. The personal relationship seemed to be real, full of love and trust and the vulnerability that was displayed was demonstrating a surrender I had never seen in Islam. Each person came here freely, lovingly, and without fear, and not for the reason of making a statement or following a requirement, but out of pure love and faith. That was obvious.

As I observed the scene before me, the guilt quickly came back in full force, reminding me of my Muslim faith and that everything before and around me was contrary to it—how silly I was to think that I had heard Mary calling me. As my mind continued the onslaught, I knew that though I admired the purity of prayer before me, I could not kneel before an idol. I felt trapped within my Islamic beliefs and culture. After sitting quietly for a while and not hearing the gentle voice again, I finally left. For the next few days of our New York visit, my heart longed to go back to the Cathedral. Simon was obviously surprised at my sudden desire to return to a place that I had initially refused to go. He was amazed that it was so important to me now, that I planned the remaining days we were there around the daily stop at St. Patrick's Cathedral. Simon didn't question me, but would leave me there alone, and take the kids, keeping them entertained at stores nearby. I would sit before Mary and my soul rested with her, and I once again experienced a deep peace. My Muslim mind somehow quieted enough to allow me to be still and soak in the peace in front of Maryam who had suddenly become Mary.

Sania was in high school now and driving, which caused me great anxiety. I couldn't understand how American kids were allowed to get their license at sixteen. It seemed to me that they were too young. I certainly didn't want my daughter to wait until she was thirty like me, but sixteen seemed too early. Sania was headstrong and independent, and she wasn't going to wait a day over sixteen to drive off to school on her own. As she grew up, the teenage challenges came along, something I had no understanding of since I never considered defying my parents and their wishes. Hamza was in middle school, and since he was a boy, I was spared the emotional highs and lows and the wardrobe fights which were frequent between Sania and me. With all life's busyness, the experience in St. Patrick's Cathedral faded in my memory, and I never dwelled upon the event. Thankfully God decided to knock on my heart again.

Soon after Thanksgiving, the same year as the New York trip, the countdown to Christmas began. Since the time of our marriage, Simon and I celebrated Christmas in the American traditions. I looked at it as a festive and joyful time abounding with sweet desserts that were my weakness, and an opportunity to show love to friends and family. I also loved having a Christmas tree and decorating it. Simon had introduced some of his family traditions to us, and one of them was each of us getting a Christmas ornament every year and new pajamas which we would wear Christmas Eve to open our presents. Simon would also make sure that everyone got a gag gift that was a source of much screams and laughter every year. I was trying hard to make memories with the children who seemed to be growing up too fast.

That year my parents were visiting from Canada, and we involved them in the fun of decorating the tree, buying presents, ornaments, and soaking in the holiday spirit. To them, it was a commercial trap, but they smiled and indulged us, trying their best to enjoy it with us. It was then, in the early part of December, that I had the first dream that changed the path of my life and led me to my greatest adventure.

It was an early December morning, and I was just coming out of deep sleep and noticed that light was starting to come in through the window next to my bed. Awakened gently, my eyes were half open, but I was not fully awake. At this time, between sleep and consciousness, I became aware of a presence on the left side by the edge of my bed. It was Jesus standing there with Mary beside Him. They were so close that they were touching the bed, just inches away from me. I could see Mary's profile as she looked at Jesus. She had a veil covering her head, and Jesus was wearing the crown of thorns. They started to speak to my soul, and a joy filled my heart. They were not speaking with audible words, but they both spoke at the same time to my soul, and in return, while they listened intently, my soul was telling them everything that was ever in my heart with the trust and abandon of a child. It was a deep conversation accomplished in silence, and an incredible peace was present. This communion seemed to go on for a long time, and after this sharing, we prayed together, and I felt a joy and peace fill me in a way I had never experienced before.

As all this was happening, a light was poured into my soul that continued to pierce me as long as they were present. Through it all, I was staring at them in love, and they returned my gaze silently. It seemed that hours passed, and as they left, I woke up filled with joy (a feeling distinct from happiness), smiling because I knew there was a light shining within me due to that encounter. Where there was once darkness, now there was a light, and I was acutely aware of it. I knew it wasn't an ordinary dream, and somehow, I was changed. Though it felt like I had been awake all night talking and praying within the depth of my soul, I felt physically rested, refreshed, and fulfilled in my spirit in a way that seems impossible to describe.

Later that morning over breakfast, I told my mother about the encounter, trying to describe the incredible feelings and change I was feeling within me. She smiled and said since it was near Christmas my mind had probably created it, and dismissed it as a good thing that I had dreamt of a Prophet and his mother. She went on to another topic, not seeing the need to discuss this further. Initially I believed she was right; I must be overthinking the dream, but I couldn't get it out of my mind and physically I felt different too.

I truly felt that I had been touched by the Divine. The explanation that dreams are visions produced by your thoughts buried into ones subconscious mind didn't seem to apply to this dream. I had been disconnected from the true meaning of Christmas; I did not think about Jesus or Mary. I was a devout Muslim, practicing more strictly than my mother. To me, Christmas was a family holiday where we exchanged gifts, and ate the many delicious desserts which I loved. I wasn't thinking about Jesus or Mary, but rather of cookies and presents!

There was no doubt in my mind that my soul had been touched and changed. Filled with wonder at what had taken place was short lived until my mind again actively entered into the picture and began questioning it in detail within my Islamic boundaries. The joy slowly gave way to confusion and fear as I struggled to push it aside. But through Mary, the birth of Jesus had already taken place in my heart, and little did I know that nothing would ever be the same again from that day onward.

The peace that was beyond understanding had filled me, and I stopped moving. I left my lover's arms and rested in the arms of a Mother as the music became softer and in harmony with my breath. In her arms, I knew I was safe from the pitfalls of the dance floor. She would lead me into the right direction. The dance with this gentle woman was effortless; I felt like I was floating as I followed her lead. She led me towards a great Light, a Light she knew well, but my feet started to get heavy and resist, fearful to enter into the unknown beauty.

CHAPTER 11

Jesus: Prophet or Messiah?

By the end of January, things settled back to the normal routine, and my parents left to go back home. I told Simon about my dream, and I explained that I knew it wasn't in my imagination. Jesus and Mary had come to visit me, and I was confused. It wasn't simply "a good sign." It felt like there was a much bigger significance and purpose. I had not allowed Simon the opportunity to discuss other religions with me until now. My questions and subsequent confusion opened the door for him to introduce me to Jesus the Messiah for the first time.

He explained that Jesus was the Son of God and that He came to redeem mankind and all who believed in Him would be saved. Jesus loved us so much that He took the sins of the world upon Himself so that we might be forgiven. As Simon explained the facts about Christianity, I could hardly stand to hear these blasphemous words! Allah was the one, the only Supreme Being, the creator of the entire universe.

Why would He need to send His Son? Why would He even need to have a Son? It made no sense to me. This God sounded like He had feelings and cared about people like a Father, and I didn't feel that way about Allah, though I loved Him. Allah was not begotten, nor did He beget. He was the one and only, who was powerful and expected us to follow His laws if we wanted to avoid Hell. Those who did not believe in Him and His messenger Mohammad were, unfortunately, going to Hell. I was torn, wanting to ask more questions about this Prophet who had appeared in my dream, but I was not able to hear about Him from a Christian perspective. From the Quran, I knew that the Prophet Isa was born to a virgin, Mariam, whom Allah had chosen to honor. Jesus was born human, though His birth was miraculous, and He grew up to perform many miracles of healing and He even raised people from the dead. His main purpose was to call people to submission to God. The Quran says that the holy book (Bible) that talks about Jesus is true but was distorted by people, and the true message lost. The *true* message of the Prophet Jesus was in full agreement with the Quran. Therefore, I couldn't trust the Bible and its teachings.

Until then, I had considered Islam and Christianity to have much in common, but now that I was learning more about Christianity from Simon, I found there were major disparities. The differences between Islam and Christianity were much deeper than just the disagreement about the Divinity of Jesus. Islam described a completely different Jesus than Christianity. According to Islam, the mission of Jesus was to preach submission to one God, whereas Christianity focused on His mission of redemption from sin and slavery to Satan through His suffering, death, and Resurrection. Islam rejects Jesus's suffering, explaining that Allah was too merciful to allow His Prophet to suffer, and instead, replaced Him with another body (Quran, Surah: 3:59, 4:157-173). Since Jesus was taken from the Cross and saved from the agony, He never died, which means there is no Resurrection, which is a central belief in Christianity. So, in short, everything Christianity stood for: the Incarnation, the Passion, the Redemption, and the Resurrection, were all denied in the Quran. Therefore, I concluded that Jesus was a holy Prophet who came to pave the way for

Mohammad by preaching monotheism and submission to God, and He would return at the end of time and reaffirm everything that Mohammad had preached and would announce that He was merely a man, not divine (Quran 5:116-117). However holy He was, He was simply a man born to a pious woman, Maryam (Quran: 19, 3:42-51). Since the Bible was corrupted, there was no other trustworthy source of information on this man Jesus.

I tried to find peace in accepting this teaching of Islam and to forget the dream that had started this discussion about Jesus. But my heart was unsettled, and I could not stop thinking about this Jesus and who He was. I knew this was not just a dream. I felt God's presence, and I knew that there was a message in this dream. I was trying hard to accept the Quran's version of Jesus, but my heart kept rebelling. I would start my day forcing myself to ignore Jesus, but by the evening I would be questioning Simon about Him, and then get angry when he would tell me about the Christian Jesus. I wanted to know more, but found it difficult to hear things that were considered blasphemous in Islam. I would be filled with fear of Allah's wrath that I was even listening about the Son of God.

Simon finally suggested that I watch the movie "The Passion of the Christ" which would help me understand Jesus's sacrifice, but I was not interested in viewing a movie not based on truth. This tug and pull continued for a few months, and through this time, my husband was my only voice of Christianity. Strangely, through this struggle I never researched anything on the computer or read any books about Christianity. All exterior influences seemed to be barred from me, and I was following only the promptings of my heart.

My dance became one that was torn between fear and love. The Light drew me, but fear pulled me back. As my ears strained to hear His voice, my heart leapt towards it, and the only one leading me in this dance was God himself.

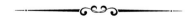

After several months of conflicting thoughts, I once again heard Mary's gentle voice in my heart. She was calling me to visit a place where she had been etched on the glass of an office building some years earlier where hundreds of spectators visited. I knew about this place from my Aunt and Uncle. Now, with only one or two visitors a day, the glass was recently vandalized but part of the image still shone through. I didn't know exactly where the building was located. The feeling persisted, so one day I decided to drive to the area and look for the shrine. I found the building and parked before the discernable image of Mary, turning off the car yet staying safely inside. After a while, I finally got out and stood before her faded silhouette.

"I'm here," I told her. "What do you want from me? What do you want me to do?"

I stood staring, and slowly I noticed that I was turned, and instead of looking at Mary, I was looking at a large statue of the Sacred Heart of Jesus, about fifteen feet away that I had not even noticed.

I couldn't take my eyes off Jesus, and I stood mesmerized for a long time, feeling that familiar deep sense of peace that I had experienced in the dream, and at St. Patrick's Cathedral. I must have spent about an hour there, turning back to Mary and asking why she called me, but in a few minutes I found myself staring at Jesus again. Eventually I left, but for the next six months, I would go there every day during my lunch hour or on my way home, spending at least an hour if not more. It became vitally important to me that I scheduled my day around this visit, drawn to go there and longing for the daily sense of rest and peace it provided.

All my years of worshipping Allah yielded nothing in return. No feelings. No peace. No love. Nothing. This was the experience I had craved all my life as I strove to become closer to God and to do His will. I was open to hearing God, but the God of my ancestors did not reveal Himself to me. Therefore, this peace that Jesus was giving me pulled me in a way that nothing else ever had, yet I was still cautious and careful not to become a fool. I erected a barrier around my heart when I was there. I shared my feelings with Simon, and he wisely let me follow my heart without too much input.

He figured that my heart was a better student than my head that only argued with everything he had tried to explain to me. I was glad, since I had difficulty explaining this feeling even to myself. However, I did know the sense of peace was real. It transcended anything else in my prayer life up to this point. Sania and Hamza witnessed the change in me as well. Now I was silent as I listened to them complain weekly about Sister Amira and her teachings about Muslims as the only ones who would go to Heaven and her insistence about no forgiveness for the unbelievers. What could I say? I was trying to figure out the answers. Slowly I stopped forcing them to pray in the evenings. They overheard some of my conversations with Simon and were happy to hear Jesus mentioned. Their secret hope by now was that "Mom would change."

I was questioning Jesus consistently. If Mary had called me but kept turning me to Jesus, well, then I was going to ask Him the questions! So, I did; I asked many questions of Him and also told Him how things should or shouldn't be!

"I know you are a Prophet, and I love and respect you, but I don't know what more you want from me. God doesn't have a son! There is no Son of God! You are a Prophet; you will come at the end of time and tell the lost Christians that there is no Trinity and that they were wrong, so why are you drawing me towards the wrong faith? What do you want? Why are you bothering and confusing me? Haven't I have gone through enough turmoil in my life, fighting for divorce and then marrying outside the culture, and now you are creating more problems for me! Why are you calling me, when it should be Mohammad?"

On and on I went, but there was no answer. Eventually I would calm down, after venting my frustrations, and slowly start to talk to

Him about my life. I shared with Him my fears and concerns regarding my teenage children, frustrations at work, and basically everything that was happening in my life. This became similar to a visit with a close friend with whom I could share everything.

Since that first dream near Christmas time, I felt as if a bubble of protection covered me, and I felt God's presence very strongly. Also, I had suddenly started to notice Jesus, the Bible, the Cross, and other Christian symbols everywhere I went, and I felt drawn to them like a magnet. Before I was blind to them, but now my eyes were open to all the Christian symbols around me that I had disregarded in the past, and it seemed like there was a glow around them.

Gentle whispers guided me in what to do and where to go, and it seemed as if nature was singing God's glory. For many years, my heart longed to be free and fly like a bird, to be free from the prison where I had no control. Now suddenly birds were evident everywhere. I would notice white birds, my eyes tracked their path, and then I would feel peace and warmth in my heart. It was as if God gave me a sign that He was present, loving, and signaling my freedom. I was perplexed by these events thinking that perhaps I imagined the amazing grace and love of God, but I felt more alive than ever. Much later I would understand the significance of the white bird as the symbol of the Holy Spirit.

I did not share any of these Christian happenings with even my close Muslim friends. During this time I met Debbie, a friend from work, and though our friendship was new, I felt drawn to tell her about the unusual events. I expected her to say something similar to my mother's remarks that my mind had created all of the things I thought I experienced, and it was probably due to my overactive imagination. But Debbie said something totally different and unexpected.

With a look of wonder, she exclaimed, "Something really special is happening to you, Naylah. It is a gift and a blessing, and not many people have them! You should come to my church!"

Well I didn't feel that my experiences were a gift at all, but rather at times I felt torn and confused between the conflicting teaching of Islam, the fear of going to Hell, and the peace and love that continued to tug at me when I went to see Jesus. Though I had become best friends with this confusing Jesus with whom I shared everything, I didn't want any pressure to join and conform to a church. I had loved the presence of God throughout my day, but I didn't want to do anything crazy like attending a church, since my fear of offending Allah was very much alive in me. I smiled at Debbie and changed the subject. I was still praying the *namaz* since I believed that was the only way to pray. I was still holding on to Islam, but now I stopped reading the Quran. Somehow, I felt no desire to read it anymore.

One day, out of the blue, I felt God urging me to watch "The Passion of the Christ." I felt Him say that it was now time to watch the movie, the same one that I refused to watch months ago at Simon's suggestion. By now I was spending much of my time with Jesus, and when I heard God's gentle prompting, I felt the desire and readiness to watch the film. Simon was elated that I finally asked to see the movie, and that weekend we went to a local video rental store. Upon arriving, Simon excitedly rushed off to look for the movie in the faith section, while I looked for a video that was a new release, and entertaining. I was willing to watch the movie, but I was not as enthusiastic as Simon. I was still confused with the direction God was leading.

Soon a very disappointed Simon informed me that the movie was not available, possibly checked out. I was relieved in a way as I had heard it was very hard to watch, and happily assured Simon not to worry, we could see it another time. I continued searching for another movie. Well, I thought, I did my part, so now it was up to God—if He wanted me to see the movie, He would make it available.

Suddenly, front-and-center in the new releases was "The Passion of the Christ"! It was if a light was shining on it and the face of Jesus seemed alive and staring right at me! I stood there shocked, and I heard a voice say, "Take it!"

As I stretched out my hand to pick it up, it seemed as if the movie nearly jumped off the shelf into my hands! By this time my hands were shaking as I held the movie, staring at it speechless.

He truly did want me to watch it! How can this be? I kept asking myself, "This is crazy!" I quickly found Simon and wordlessly handed him the movie, and he looked at me, his expression mirroring my shock.

"Where did you get this? I looked everywhere and couldn't find it," he said.

My mouth was dry, and I could barely form the words as I recounted the events. He saw my dazed look and understood. We quickly paid for the rental and headed home in silence. As believers in God, we say that He is involved in our lives and watches over us, but when God starts to show us that He is truly involved, it becomes unnerving and is often out of our comfort zone!

Usually I would worry when the kids went out at night, but that night I was glad that we had privacy to watch the movie. I watched "The Passion of the Christ," without uttering a word as tears rolled down my face through most of the movie as I watched the suffering of Jesus and Mary. I felt like my heart was pierced with pain as it seemed that Jesus was communicating His agony to me personally through this film. I cried as I felt He was seeking a friend to console Him. To say I was deeply affected is an understatement. I walked His bitter Passion united with Jesus and Mary, and I connected with Him on a much deeper, more spiritual level. At the end, I felt God saying, "Do you understand now?"

That night, the question about the truth of His suffering was gone. I knew it was true. Jesus had suffered and died on the Cross and rose again. I believed that deep in my heart now. My past Islamic belief on this issue – that Jesus as a Prophet of God who had been spared the suffering-- was no longer true for me.

I questioned myself—was I creating a truth based on my feelings? But I knew I was not making it up, this was beyond my feelings, it just was! Sometimes we create "truth" for our convenience and desires, but this realization was very inconvenient for me to accept. It wasn't making things easier for me. It was being revealed to me with no effort on my part since I was still a reluctant participant!

After watching the movie, when I visited Him at the shrine, it was different. I felt I was visiting a friend whom I knew intimately, and as I looked at Him now, I was in awe of the love that led Him to suffer and be crucified. But I didn't understand His love for me personally yet.

I was slowly forming a relationship with Jesus of Nazareth. He had become my friend through His mother's introduction, and He was no longer a dead Prophet or a historical figure. He had come alive for me, and I knew He was with me, and while my intellect had a difficult time making sense of this, my heart knew it without a doubt. But how was this possible? I knew that He had lived 2,000 years ago and had died, so how was I feeling His presence today? Though I had not reconciled the Christian Jesus with the Muslim Jesus, I had unknowingly started to fall in love with Him.

The music had slowed and changed to a love duet with a haunting melody. Oh, what love was this, which was causing my heart to ache and thirst at the same time? How could I ever be the same as this love was being poured upon me?

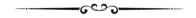

CHAPTER 12

The Search

The dreams, as well as the visions continued, and they all pointed to Jesus. One of those dreams was especially significant because it left me changed, in the same way as the first one. In this dream, I saw myself climbing a curving set of stairs with a woman whom I knew. The stairs represented a change of religion. As we both climbed upwards, there were people standing at the bottom which included my friends and family. They were screaming "No! Don't do it! Don't leave the religion!"

We ignored them and continued up the steps until we reached the top which opened to a flat rooftop. As we stepped out onto the roof, there was total silence and peace as the screams and shouts from the bottom had faded away. I saw people walking in twos and threes, traveling in different directions, yet they seemed to be in harmony, conversing, although I couldn't hear anything. My companion and I started to walk together towards a certain direction. I knew it represented a religion, and as we were walking, I felt a light touch on my right shoulder to signal me to stop. The friend continued walking.

As I turned, I saw the whitest and brightest light before me, and from that light were rays of immense love flowing, the rays seemed alive and pulsating as they touched me. I felt like I was going to faint. I could hardly bear the intensity of this incredible, unimaginable love. My soul wanted to go into the Light and drown in the love, but as I began to lean forward feeling like I was going to lose consciousness, a hand came out of the Light to give me something. I extended my hands and in it floated down a scapular with the Sacred Heart of Jesus and the Immaculate Heart of Mary. As I looked at it and held it, the Light faded away.

All the understanding of love that I had seen, dreamt, or read about in any romance novel seemed like a cheap version in comparison to the love I had experienced in this dream. The purity and power of this love were beyond words. I woke up knowing that what I had experienced was not just a dream; I had truly encountered this Light, and the ecstasy of my soul in the presence of this Light was a real experience. I was left thirsting for this love and the desire to be in this Light forever. And again, on that strange-looking threaded necklace were images of Jesus and Mary, and once again, no sign of Mohammad!

The next morning I returned to the outdoor shrine, sitting before the statue of Jesus and image of Mary. The ladies who managed the shrine were playing a digital recording of prayers and songs that I found soothing. They gave me prayer beads with a card, inviting me to say the prayers along with the recording. They told me the prayer was called the Rosary. I particularly liked the "Our Father" prayer and I had no problem calling God Father, even though it was blasphemous for a Muslim to do so as it brings a mere human being in relationship with the Almighty God.

By now I had lost count of how many sins I was committing according to Islam. I started reading the "Hail Mary," but came to a screeching halt at the words, "Holy Mary, Mother of God, pray for us sinners now and at the hour of our death." I could never utter the words "Mother of God." I was not going to offend Allah further, although I couldn't figure out why He was allowing this relationship with Jesus completely outside the Islamic parameters. I compromised by saying the first half of the "Hail Mary," and stubbornly refused to say the last part that included "Holy Mary, Mother of God, pray for us sinners now and at the hour of our death."

A year passed, and it was December again, with the Christmas spirit in the air. By now I had stopped Sister Amira's classes for the children, much to the delight of Sania and Hamza, and instead this Christmas season, the meaning of Christmas and Jesus was discussed at our table. Sania and Hamza were happily devouring cookies and listening raptly to Simon, finally free to tell Christmas stories. What a change over the last year and it had only brought peace within each of our hearts.

During this Christmas season, I went to lunch with Debbie, my new friend who had invited me to her church. She gave me a beautiful, blessed Christmas Rosary as a Christmas gift. She explained she was sending rosaries to Haiti, but she thought it was important for me to have one. Later she shared that she felt that I was experiencing something special in my life and that I needed guidance beyond her understanding. Knowing the promises of the rosary, she hoped between my using it and her prayers for me that I would be guided on the right path. Again, she invited me to her church, promising that I would enjoy it. I thanked her for the beautiful rosary, completely unaware that it was a traditional Catholic prayer. I stubbornly refused to use the Internet for any research during my entire journey of faith, desiring only to be totally led by God, His promptings, and through dreams and visions. I had no understanding of the different denominations of Christianity and had no idea that all my dreams and visions, including the shrine, were all of Catholic significance. My time at the Catholic school in Indiana obviously had no impact on my knowledge of Catholicism!

That year Simon asked me if we wanted to go to a Christmas service at a church since he knew that my interest in Jesus had intensified over the past year. I agreed as I felt ready to take the next step. It was time to take my relationship with Jesus to the next level, and I needed some answers. I thought if I went to a church, the house of Jesus, maybe He would speak and tell me what He wanted from me. Simon suggested a church near our house that was having a candlelight service on Christmas Eve, as he thought that it would be an introduction to Christianity for me, and I happily agreed. The children knew about my dreams by now, and to them, this was our way to understand more about Jesus who had saved them from the Islamic teacher! They thought Jesus was pretty awesome in the way He had changed their mother's mind, something they had never thought could happen.

As I shopped and prepared that Christmas, my heart felt a deep joy and excitement that I had not experienced in the previous seasons. The anticipation of the Christ Child was filling my heart with wonder, though I had still not accepted Him as the Messiah. My heart raced ahead of my mind, which was fighting every step of the way on this journey by instilling fears and doubts.

When Christmas Eve finally arrived, we shared laughter over the gag gifts and the many other gifts that filled the bottom of the tree. Soon it was time for the Christmas Midnight Service. I was nervous with anticipation as I was taking a big step by going "public," because I had never freely chosen to attend a gathering of another religion. I was excited and scared and partly feeling guilty.

The parking lot was pretty full when we got there, and as we walked in I could see that the people were also feeling the joy of the night. It felt good to be in the company of a community that knew and loved Jesus since until now, my feelings had been secret and hidden, as I had continued to associate with my Muslim friends. In the church there were chairs placed around the podium, and we found a spot near the middle. I looked at the children, and they seemed comfortable. I felt a little self-conscious as if everyone there knew we were Muslims, but the feeling soon passed as no one stared at us. Soon we were all handed candles, and the pastor came forward and introduced himself. He did a reading from the Bible and gave a sermon. Soon after, they passed around a tray of bread and plastic cups with grape juice. I didn't understand the significance of it, but participated in it.

After that, we all proceeded down the aisle singing with our lit candles that ended the service. As I stood outside, I felt empty and a bit disappointed. I wasn't sure what I was expecting, but I knew that something was missing. As we walked to the car, Simon excitedly asked me, "So, what did you think?"

"It was a beautiful service, but The One Who Is Calling Me wasn't there." As these words fell out of my mouth, I was frustrated. I had finally gone to a Christian church and attended a service—but I did not feel His presence! Simon looked as frustrated as me. He didn't understand why I was making this so difficult. What more did I want? I didn't have the answer myself, but I clearly knew that the emptiness and yearning that I felt in my soul had not been satisfied that night. Where would I go to find this Jesus since I didn't encounter him in His church?

I was finally stepping towards the Light, but my Beloved was hiding from me. I moved closer savoring the sweet love melody, desperately longing for a glimpse of my Beloved. Oh, my Love, where have you gone?

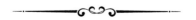

The New Year was ushered in, and I was back to my routine of work, children, and vigil at the shrine. I had outgrown the parking lot at the building, sitting before the images of Jesus and Mary alone, and I knew I needed more. But where was I supposed to go? I had no idea what to do next. My dear, persistent friend Debbie invited me again when I told her about my disappointment over the Christmas Eve service. This time I was ready, and I agreed to go, but on one condition. I wanted to go when there was no service. After all, The One Who Was Calling Me might not be at this church either, and I didn't want to be stuck in a service for no reason.

I was frustrated with myself! Why couldn't I be satisfied at that church on Christmas Eve like all of the other people there who seemed to be so happy and at peace? But Debbie seemed pretty confident that I would find The One Who Was Calling Me in her church. I met Debbie at the church parking lot one morning, and I was happy to see that there were no other cars. It was a beautiful large building, and the sign said St. Ignatius Roman Catholic Church. We walked in, and I remember stepping into the building, taking a deep breath, and immediately thinking, *He is here! The One Who Has Been Calling Me is here!* His presence hit me strongly.

My soul felt relief; it had finally arrived at Jesus's home. But my mind, as usual, was off on its own, looking around, listening to Debbie and preparing arguments to reject Jesus. We sat in the pew together silently, and I felt peace and knew that I was finally in the right place. This is where God had been calling me, and Jesus was present. This was His home. I could feel Him!

I knew from that moment that this church was where I was supposed to go and continue my search. I started going to that church every day, but only when it was empty. I didn't want anyone to push their faith on me or tell me what I should or shouldn't believe. I wanted to hear from God who had been leading me on this journey, but now seemed to have gone silent! So I sat there, staring at the large wooden crucifix in the front and continued questioning Jesus.

"Well I am here; I don't know what you want from me. I know you are a great Prophet and I know you suffered tremendously, but you are definitely NOT the Son of God—may Allah forgive me for even saying such a blasphemous thing! You can't be the Son of God because there is NO Son of God! Allah, my God, I don't know what you are doing, but I am tired of this. I do not want to displease you, so please explain this mystery of Jesus. Please send me a dream about the Prophet Mohammad and allow this to make sense."

Eventually, my rant quieted down and then I would stare at the crucifix and again start speaking to Jesus as if He were my best friend. I believed in His suffering and so felt that He could understand mine and I would recount all that was on my heart that day: my worries, fears, and questions about my daily life. I usually left after an hour or two, no longer frustrated, but instead feeling peace and comfort. I had no idea that was one of Jesus's promises in the Bible: *"Come to me, all you who labor and are burdened, and I will give you rest"* (Matthew 11:28).

This Jesus had become my confidante and my best friend, and I was glad that at least I could finally meet Him in His house. Months went by, and the routine was the same, until one day I was again going through my frustrated arguments, explaining why I could not worship Him as the Son of God and asking Allah for forgiveness.

I was sitting in my usual pew near the back of the church, alone—looking at the crucifix above the Tabernacle saying, "Who do you think you are? You can't be the Son of God because there is NO son of God! Allah is all powerful and the only one."

Jesus decided to answer me that day. Suddenly, I heard Him speak from the direction of the Crucifix and Tabernacle, "Who are *YOU*, to tell Me who I can be and cannot be? If you REALLY want to know the Truth, go! And come back like a child, and I will tell you the Truth!"

It was an audible voice, and it had a power and authority that left me shaking and speechless. When I was able to move, I ran out of the church, not sure what had just happened. But as I collected myself and caught my breath, I knew without a doubt what I had heard, and from Whom I had heard it, and I understood exactly what He was saying to me. The words seared into my mind. I had to erase my family's teachings about my faith and culture for forty years as a Muslim, and I must come before Him innocent and pure as a child with a teachable spirit. He would then reveal the Truth to me. I had to empty myself of the rules I had been taught by Man so that God could teach me His Truth. The condemning voices in my head had to be silenced so I could hear the voice of God.

I struggled with that thought—how was I to erase all that I knew about Allah and be open as a child? How was I to silence the voice in my head that told me what to do and believe? All of the teaching of my youth, all of the fear of God, had to change. At the same time, I had been thirsting for the Truth for so long that I couldn't walk away. I knew there was an objective truth that existed that was not at the mercy of Man and his selfish desires and interpretations. I wanted that pure and holy Truth, and I knew full well that it would come with a price.

As I swayed to the love song, drawn to my Beloved, I knew that once I walked into His arms, I would be completely His. It would cost me all that was familiar to me. Would I be strong enough to abandon all that was familiar?

PART 3

LIGHT

"I am the Light of the World, Whoever follows Me will not walk in Darkness but will have The Light of Life."

— John 8:12

CHAPTER 13

Meeting Truth

The next day, I gathered my courage and went back to church. Alone, I sat in my usual pew and took a deep breath. I closed my eyes, and amazingly at that moment, all became silent—in my heart and in my head. The nagging and argumentative voice in my mind that never let my heart rest was suddenly quiet. In that window of silence, I finally put aside my Muslim faith and beliefs. By God's grace, I truly sat before God as an innocent child with a teachable spirit. I opened my eyes and looked at the crucifix, and said "OK, I am here, completely open. I don't know anything. Now you tell me the Truth." I didn't know if I was speaking to Jesus or God, but strangely they seemed to have become One.

As soon as I said that, a bolt of light came from the direction of the Cross and pierced my heart, and in an instant, my mind was illuminated with the Truth. It was as if the wall that had been there between God and me came crashing down, and in an instant, I knew the Truth! Jesus was the Son of God. He was the Lord, the Son of the Father, who came to save me! He was the Truth! I knew it!

I fell to my knees for the first time before Him, sobbing and unable to bear the love that was being poured out over me, and my mind and heart were screaming in unison for the first time, "I believe You are the Christ, the Son of God. I believe!" The words of Scripture were coming alive in my life: *At the Name of Jesus every knee should bend, of those in heaven and on earth, and under the earth, and every tongue confess that Jesus Christ is Lord, to the Glory of God the Father* (Philippians 2:10).

I felt like an ocean of love was flooding over me, and I knew it was the love of God the Father. The moment I accepted Jesus, I had met God the Father. He wasn't Allah, and He wasn't just God, He was God the Father because I felt the love for His Son and Their love for me. Words fail to describe that moment.

How could I describe the love of the One who is Love Himself, and this incredible relationship between the Father and the Son that was being infused into me? Truth was revealed to me in a moment that day, answering the burning thirst.

Jesus was the Truth!

At that moment so much was accomplished in my faith, my spirit, and my soul simultaneously. It was just like that first dream where no words were spoken, but rather it was a much deeper communication. God had revealed the Truth to my soul! The wall of darkness I had previously felt between me and God came crashing down, and I met Abba for the first time. My soul could barely contain the ecstasy of this meeting. The feelings were different than what I had learned or experienced about Allah. I was finally experiencing the God that my heart had always believed in, He was different than Allah. Allah was a supreme creator and master who was removed from human beings, but this presence of God was not the same — He was my Father; it was personal! I was filled with a pure love for I realized for the first time that God had only one name-LOVE. Through Jesus, I met God the Father and tasted His love! Again, Scripture was being fulfilled without my knowing! *"I am the way, and the truth, and the life. No one comes to the Father except through me"* (John 14:6).

All these years I had longed to know the Father, but what I didn't know was that Jesus was the doorway to God. That day was a blessed day, the day that I was saved, and my soul rejoiced in this gift of salvation. I left the church in a daze, my mind not able to grasp what had happened. I began an adventure and entered a mystery that was beyond my understanding.

That evening I shared with my husband what took place, as best as I could, but I had a difficult time articulating my experience. My soul was rejoicing, and it was ecstatic and free for the first time. But soon my mind returned in full force to its old condemning and questioning self. The whispers and questions rebelled against the Truth that now rested in my soul.

I was tormented by these thoughts: "Are you sure this happened? Maybe you created all this in your mind. Maybe you are losing your mind! How can this be? So, does this mean that Islam is wrong? What if you are being misled? What if this is from the Devil?"

The whispers became louder and louder until it was a constant screaming in my head. It seemed a war was taking place between my soul and my mind. My soul continued to feel joy, peace, and conviction whereas my mind was refusing to submit and it continued to torment me. I saw my Beloved standing before me, and my heart soaked in His love. He stood smiling before me, waiting for me to run into His arms as the music continued its soothing melody. But my feet were frozen, refusing to move, Fear holding me in its grip.

"Faith is to believe what you do not see; the reward of this faith is to see what you believe."

– *St. Augustine*

111

I was confused once again, but the difference this time was that I no longer denied Jesus Christ was the Son of God. I knew that He was the Truth, but the uncertainty of where this path would take me filled me with fear. I suddenly started to feel the presence of evil which became so strong that it was palpable. I could feel its fury and scorn towards me for turning towards Christ, something that I had never encountered while I practiced Islam.

I always believed as a Muslim that Satan existed, but now I felt his anger and hatred! It was scary, and I felt so alone trying to make sense of it, and lonely, for how could I ever explain this to anyone? I had no physical proof to show what I was feeling, just as I had no proof of my experience with God. But I was very clear about the difference between the two: with one, I felt God's presence, His love, peace, and a deep sense of joy, whereas with Satan's presence I felt hatred, anxiety, and fear.

He haunted me with images of me in a mental asylum and my children looking at me, and I could see what was going through their mind and feel their pain, as well as my anguish as I gazed at them through the bars. I was reminded that I was there because of following Jesus. A voice would threaten me, "This was where you would end up if you don't stop this Jesus nonsense!" The silky, evil voice would taunt me reminding me, how much pain I had caused my parents and my children by divorcing Tahir, and how I had been horribly selfish. How could I now start down this path of Christianity as it would certainly devastate my parents! The accusations continued endlessly, the voice so full of disgust that I could physically feel how repulsive I was to it.

Another repeating vision showed my funeral with no one there to mourn my passing. My body was lying outside while a stormy wind blew sand over my still form, the same voice saying, "Nobody cares about you and this is how you will end up, ALONE, if you pursue this path!" Once again, I felt the hatred and disgust from the voice tha accompanied the vision.

The painful visions and taunting voice that tormented me had to be from the devil, because it used fear and anger to manipulate me. I had felt hounded by God when He first started to call me, but He never accused or tried to exert control over me. God extended an invitation of love, leaving me free to choose, whereas this was driven by fear and hate. The devil knew all the right buttons to push as he was familiar with my past wounds and fears, and he exploited them, throwing in a kernel of truth into his lies to confuse me. It was a very hard battle that was keeping me from making any decisions.

These spiritual attacks kept stirring my fears, as I knew that choosing Jesus would cost me my friends and possibly my family. My social life would be shaken to the core. Even though most of my friends were moderates, they believed, as most Muslims did, that apostasy was the worst sin. They would never understand. How could they? I barely understood and believed the events leading up to this moment myself!

I belonged to a culture where religion and tradition were so intertwined, that leaving the religion would most assuredly leave me on the outer circle of society. My family was liberal, so I knew that they would not condemn me, but I knew what my Muslim friends would think of me, and they would blame my parents for failing to raise me correctly. I knew this would be very difficult for my parents and would cause even more pain. I also knew my sisters would face questions from their families, and my children would suffer the effects as well with family and friends. This step would cause a ripple effect much further than me, and because of my love for my family I struggled with the decision. Simon appeared to support me and said that religion was personal, but I didn't want to cause more turmoil and pain as things had finally settled into a routine for us. At the same time, I couldn't deny my faith in Jesus either!

While my mind vacillated through all the pros and cons, Satan took advantage of my anguish and continued with his accusations. The bright spot in this struggle was that my love for Jesus stayed strong and drew me to church every day. By now I attended Mass at the church. Strangely enough, I still had not touched the computer for any research on Christianity, I had not read a word from the Bible, and I had no idea what the Catholic Church taught. All my instruction revealed to my spirit was only by God. I knew it was God, because of the deep love, peace, and joy I experienced when He spoke, and the authority He spoke with never left me in any doubt it was God. I felt a sense of order; things were how they were supposed to be when I attended Mass.

One morning at church as I sat in my usual spot in the last pew, I noticed that the priest was African. I could tell by his accent that was familiar to me since I had spent many years in Africa. He was reading from the Gospel of John: "If you remain in my word, you will truly be my disciples, and you will know the truth, and the truth will set you free."

As I heard the words, I felt they were alive and were piercing me. I felt like my body was on fire, and Jesus was standing before me. He was speaking to me! I started to shake and cry, unable to bear His presence. I knew what He was saying. He had revealed the Truth to me, the Truth that I had asked for, but I was still in bondage to fear. The Truth had to be lived freely and publicly. I felt ashamed and convicted at the same time. How beautiful was this Jesus who only asked for love, using no force or fear, and stood before me waiting! My heart could barely take His overpowering love and I desired to give all of myself to Him in return! I had to! I couldn't turn away from His love!

The priest was a powerful preacher, and that only increased the burning within me. I wanted to be this beautiful disciple of Jesus. I wanted to be free! The Mass ended and I sat glued in my seat, unable to move, sobbing and overwhelmed with love. Father Greg, the priest, walked by me and was on his way out of the church. At that moment, as he went by, I made my decision. I was going to follow Jesus! I ran after him, and as I caught him just outside the door, I could barely get the words out between the sobs. What a sight I must have been to him and the people leaving the church! Thankfully he didn't turn away from me thinking I was crazy, but listened to me patiently as I blurted out that I was Muslim and some broken sentences about dreams and visions of Jesus.

He seemed calm as I tried to explain the amazing events through my tears, and he simply smiled and said, "Why don't we go to my office and we can continue our conversation."

That day, between tears and smiles, I shared with him my journey that had brought me to this church. "I only wanted to follow Allah, I wanted to know Him, but instead I found Jesus! I am totally in love with Him. I come to this church every day because I love Him so much, and I know He is here!"

I poured out my heart completely, as I explained about the dreams that had transformed me and were forever etched in my heart and mind, holding nothing back. After about two hours of sharing, he invited me to come back to continue our discussion. Father Greg was a visiting priest from Nigeria, and he did not have the normal obligations of a pastor, and this allowed him to give me the time I needed over the next few weeks. He listened well and explained about the teachings of Christ. I soaked it in, feeling like a thirst of forty years was finally being quenched. Little did I know that this Jesus who I was so in love with had spoken about it 2,000 years ago: *"But whoever drinks the water I shall give will never thirst; the water I shall give will become in him a spring of water welling up to eternal life"* (John 4:14).

Finally one day, Father Greg asked me what I thought God was asking me. I knew the answer—He was asking me to choose to step out of my familiar Muslim faith and follow Him, who was Truth itself. I had asked for it, begged for it, and He had personally come to reveal it to me in an incredible way. Now I needed to make a choice. I knew that only by following the Truth could I be free. If I followed Him, I could fly like the birds. But the choice was mine.

I am not sure when I came to think of Jesus as God, but the Truth had quietly rooted itself in my heart. I knew He was God, because only God could love like He loved me, even after my rejection. Only God could touch my spirit and infuse the Truth in such a gentle way, and fill me with such peace. Only God could have the magnanimous love to suffer for even those who didn't love Him, and open the door to Heaven for all mankind! And finally, only God could have turned me around from my faith in Islam to accept the very things that were once blasphemous to me!

I discovered the most unusual love, a love that I never read about in all the romances I had read (and I had read many!). The novels described an exclusive love, but this love I was feeling was unique, and I didn't mind sharing Jesus with the whole world. I felt even happier sharing Him, and I wanted the whole world to love Him because I realized how much He loved them! How strange and unexplainable was this love.

At Mass, when I witnessed Him being worshiped by everyone there, my heart rejoiced even more, and I felt the love multiplied. I didn't want Jesus just for myself; I wanted to share Him with the world! The best romance faded in comparison to this amazing love story in which I had suddenly entered, "I have to follow Him; I want to follow Him."

Father Greg smiled as he heard me finally make my choice. He knew how hard this was for me since he was from Nigeria and familiar with Islam where he had personally encountered the Muslim faith. Due to his experience, Father Greg understood my fears much better than an American priest ever could. He understood what my conversion to Christianity would cost me. While he helped deepen my understanding of Jesus, he never touched my freedom throughout the process, always leaving the choice up to me, confirming that I was in the right place. If Jesus didn't take away my free will and respect it, then a person who came in His Name would also have to mirror a similar trait; Father Greg demonstrated this attribute throughout our discussions, and that day I made my choice to become a Christian.

Once I made my decision, Father Greg explained that to be a Catholic, there were classes that I would be required to attend. It was important to understand the faith and to be sure it was what I wanted. He advised me to meet the director of RCIA, (the Rite of Catholic Initiation for Adults), who would explain the process further. At this point, I still didn't understand the various Christian denominations and what made each different, but I knew without a doubt that this was exactly where God wanted me. The One Who Was Calling Me was in this Catholic Church, and I felt Him every time I walked in.

Simon supported my decision as did my children. Simon had witnessed the Islamic faith and culture closely, and he had become more and more uncomfortable in that environment, even reluctant eventually to attend the parties. To him, the fear-driven and oppressive culture, even in the moderate circles, was obvious. I, on the other hand, had lived it my whole life, albeit struggling with some of the same frustrations, and failed to identify why I had been uncomfortable as quickly as he did. I was also afraid of letting go of everything familiar, as to embrace Christianity I would lose everything of which I knew and that was a part of my identity.

It was fear that Simon could not understand as he had always been graced with freedom his whole life. The Islamic faith that Simon attempted to approach with an open mind made no sense to him because he knew Jesus and His teachings. The Islamic faith and Mohammad's example had fallen painfully short. Islam had worked in reverse and led to a reaffirmation of his Christian faith, so when I finally told Simon of my decision, he was relieved!

I shared my dreams and the other extraordinary events that were leading me to Jesus with my sisters. Zara and Maira loved me, and after their initial shock, they supported me in my decision. They had witnessed my suffering for so long that they just wanted to see me happy. The most difficult hurdle was telling my parents. While I didn't want to cause them additional pain, I had no choice if I wanted to become a Christian. It was important for me to be honest and upfront. I respected them, and I had no desire to begin this journey by lying or hiding such an important change in my life. I truly wanted to share my joy. My parents happened to be visiting during this time, so I spoke to them in person. I started with the way Mary called me and pointed me to Jesus and the way He entered my life.

It was important for me to reassure them that my love for God, which I knew was important to them as well, was only deeper and more intense. I expected them to ask how I knew this was from God, or if I was being misled, which they did. I explained that if I was being led towards God with a deep desire to serve Him and purify myself, how could that be from any other source but God? The Devil would not lead me to interior cleansing and purification. Though I had searched for Allah for so long and had tried to be faithful, He never revealed what Jesus was showing me with so much love and tenderness. I wanted to reassure them that I loved God, and was becoming a better person even though the path was different. My parents listened to everything I had to say, but still could not understand why I couldn't stay Muslim, since Jesus was recognized as a Prophet in Islam.

"You can continue your relationship with God and Jesus. Why do you have to change your religion?" They asked with deep pain on their faces. "You can go to the church if it makes you happy, but please remain Muslim. Please don't abandon Islam. After a while, you might realize this is wrong, and you will be rejected by the society and religion."

As I expected, they questioned if this change was caused by my vivid imagination and if I was reading too much into my experiences. They also brought up the questions that were similar to my deepest fears: what about the family, my children, loneliness, and then finally their pain and the humiliation this would cause. We discussed these issues over the next couple of weeks, and every conversation ended with the same plea, "Just don't leave Islam."

I was finally taking a step towards my Beloved, feeling His love drawing me closer. The voices I had known my whole life kept calling me back, but I let the love song fill my ears, and my eyes stayed fixed on Him as I moved forward.

CHAPTER 14

The Choice

How could I explain the power that I was experiencing? I couldn't keep this a secret; my heart was bursting. I wanted to shout to the world that I was in love with Jesus, and I wanted to live my life with Him in the center! To me, Jesus was no longer a Prophet; He was The Son of God! He had revealed this truth to me in a personal revelation, and now I knew the Truth!

Through Jesus's atoning and redeeming sacrifice, I was adopted as a daughter of the Father. This realization led me to remember the teaching on adoption in Islam that was completely different. In Islam, it is unlawful to include an adopted child in a will. An adopted child has no claim to inheritance or the name of the family. They only receive shelter and care. (Quran 8:75) I remembered a Muslim friend of mine who was adopting a child and had been saddened to discover this teaching. The Islamic teaching never would allow the separation to be forgotten or erased. In stark contrast to this measured love, God the Father had adopted me as his daughter as soon as I had accepted His Son, and poured out His limitless love upon me.

I remembered my strong Muslim faith, which no human being could have persuaded me to leave. But Jesus and Mary had entered my life, completely changing my direction and leading me to the Way and the Truth. They showed me how I could be a part of God's family. I loved my parents deeply, and I was devastated that once again my actions caused them pain. Nothing I could say reassured them enough to see the Joy and the Light that I experienced. I understood how they felt because if I had not encountered Jesus Christ personally, I too would feel the same way. Finally, after exhausting every possible explanation, I told them, "I love you, but I have first to be obedient to God, and by rejecting what has been happening to me, I would be rejecting God."

They were saddened and hurt by my choice, and it pained me greatly to see them blame themselves for not instilling in me a deeper Muslim faith to withstand the onslaught of Christianity. They left soon after to return to Canada, and though we loved each other, our relationship became strained for several years.

I explained to my children, now in their teens, about my decision to join the Catholic Church and attend instruction at the RCIA classes. I explained that Simon and I didn't want them to feel pressured to convert or even go to church. They were free to make their decision. They both agreed that Christianity appealed to them as well, but I told them to take their time before making any decision.

Maji was living with Uncle Aslam and Aunty Naseem, and one day I shared my experience with her of Jesus and the joy that I was experiencing. She said if I was feeling closer to God and all was well at home with my children, I shouldn't worry about people. "You can never satisfy people, so you might as well do what is right for you." Again she proved herself to be wise and much more courageous than most women in that culture.

I started my RCIA classes on Monday evenings, and that became the highlight of my week. I couldn't wait to go and learn about Jesus and His Church. Soon my son Hamza said that after much consideration, he too wanted to become Catholic. He was sixteen, and he seemed sure about his decision, so a few weeks later we were in the same RCIA class. Sania, who was twenty by now, had started attending a non-denominational church and chose to be baptized there, and I was glad that she too had accepted Jesus as Lord and Savior. Through my conversion process, I had discovered EWTN (The Eternal Word Television Network), a Catholic television channel, and I was so hungry and starving to learn everything about Jesus that I watched it as much as I could.

As I listened to the different programs like *Life on the Rock, The Journey Home, Women of Grace, Mother Angelica*, and so much more, I found my heart and mind were finally fed. Finally, I was not reacting with the typical unsettled feeling to what I was hearing. At last I did not have to ignore or skip over the teachings of my faith as I did in Islam. Instead, my heart was resting in peace, absorbing what it was hearing and recognizing it as Truth.

As my heart rejoiced in finding God, the Church was reeling with clergy scandals. Soon in the midst of my newly found joy in the Catholic Church, I came face to face with the accusations and pain of the victims. It seemed at that time that the devil was mocking me and my choice to stand for this faith that was smeared in the news with ugly accusations. I saw and heard everything about these acts of sin and carried a heavy weight in my heart. Praying, I asked God, "How could this happen?" I had no doubt about the authenticity of the Catholic Church, but I didn't understand the behavior of the leaders of His church.

By God's grace, this didn't lead to a crisis in my new belief since He gave me the understanding that the issue was not with the Church instituted by Jesus. The scandal was due to the sinful choices of these apostles, and the Church suffered the consequences. Satan was hard at work tempting people, and he got the most pleasure when he succeeded in making Jesus's shepherds fall. Jesus did not take away free will, so sin, unfortunately, was still alive in the world. He was exposing the sin to the light so it could rise into the open to be addressed and purged and eventually bring healing. As it says in Ephesians 5:11-14: *"Take no part in the fruitless works of darkness; rather expose them, for it is shameful even to mention the things done by them in secret; but everything exposed by the light becomes visible for everything that becomes visible is light."*

While this failure of His shepherds was filling the news, Jesus was revealing to me how His heart was being pierced. It was a betrayal by a kiss all over again! My heart broke at the pain Jesus was experiencing, and instead of abandoning Him, I started to pray for the clergy and the victims. I realized the Devil attacked the shepherd to scatter the sheep, and he was prowling around like a lion to devour the weakest sheep.

I didn't have the answers to this sad situation, but I knew that the answer for me was not to lose faith in His Church. I felt that He was asking me as He had asked His disciples, "Will you too leave me?" And I answered from my heart as they did, "Lord, where will we go? You have the words of everlasting life." After forty years parched and in the desert, I was not leaving the living water that I had found!

The dance of joy was clouded by the ugliness of the world, yet as I swayed to the rhythm, slowly moving towards my Beloved, I knew in my heart that He would overcome this Darkness.

One day after Mass I noticed a sign saying, "Adoration on Friday." I wondered what "adoration" meant and decided to see. It was the first Friday of the month, and I went to the chapel after Mass, intrigued by the word. As I entered the small chapel, I knew this was something special. There was an air of reverence, silence, and it seemed that those seated were expectant, preparing for something important to happen. In a few minutes, the chapel was full, and the deacon walked in, dressed in his priestly robes.

As everyone knelt, he opened the tabernacle and took out the Host, encased in a gold case, which he brought to the altar and placed in the Monstrance, so all could see. He turned the Monstrance to us, and everyone started to sing a Latin worship hymn, *"O Salutaris Hostia."* I followed along. As I listened to the singing and looked at the Monstrance with Jesus in the Host, I felt transported into Heaven. My heart was dancing in my chest and overflowing with love for Him who was so humbly present in the Bread, so we could kneel before Him.

How could this be? My mind cried out, unable to comprehend, but I remembered His words to me that day from the Cross, when He asked, "Who are you to tell Me who I can be or cannot be?" So today, who was I to say what He could or should do? He was God, and if He chose to be present in a simple Host because He loved us and had promised that He would be with us until the end of time, then it was so! In John's gospel, Jesus told us that He was the Bread from Heaven, and here He was before me!

As I prayed that day, I knew that I was in the presence of God in a special way, and it was a deep and powerful experience. I could not deny how strongly I felt His presence in that consecrated bread.

How perfect was the word "Adoration." Kneeling before Him, I felt adoration was exactly what my heart was doing. From that day onward, I looked forward to the next time for Adoration! I couldn't wait to adore Him and tell Him how much I loved Him.

In the coming months, I noticed that whenever I would pray for my husband, I would immediately hear God ask me for a name. I would pray, "God, please bless my husband," and I would be stopped with the question, "Give me a name." I would answer, "Simon," and then felt I could continue with my prayer. This happened every time I prayed for Simon and I was frustrated—why did an all-knowing God keep asking me for a name? Didn't He know the name of my husband? Suddenly it hit me—He was asking for a name because He did not recognize Simon as my husband! Our marriage was not a marriage in God's eyes! I knew that we had to get married in the Church right away. Every day that went by after that realization, I understood was a day I was spending outside of God's Law. We had been married in the mosque to receive Allah's blessings, but obviously, God was telling me that He had not recognized it, and we were not married in His eyes! I had to come to the Church where He dwelt and received His blessing.

I explained to Simon that we should get married in the Church, and he agreed. I talked to Father Greg, who happened to be back in town, and he told me that we should talk to the Pastor and he would be happy to marry us. We met with the Pastor, Father Joe, and I recounted my experience in prayer, requesting that we be married in the Catholic Church. Father Joe added that not only could we get married in the Church, but I could receive all the Sacraments the same day as long as I would continue to attend RCIA classes to complete the course. As I heard these words, I was speechless, and then I started to cry. I had been longing to be baptized and to receive Jesus in Holy Communion and had prepared myself to wait for a year as I went through RCIA. But Father Joe was giving me this huge gift, and I couldn't believe it. I knew in my heart that through Father Joe, Jesus was giving me this gift in response to my deep thirst and desire to be united to Him that I could barely contain!

We filled out the paperwork to start the process of annulling our previous marriages, and Father Joe said that if the paperwork was completed in time, Father Greg could celebrate our marriage along with administering all the other Sacraments before he left for Nigeria. I couldn't believe the gifts God was giving me! I wanted Father Greg to celebrate the sacraments with us since he had been so close to me through this journey, but we had less than a month before he returned to Nigeria. Simon and I filled out the paperwork, and I prayed it would all come back in time. Within three weeks, we were free to get married in the church!

On September 13, I was baptized, confirmed, received Holy Communion, as Simon and I were married in the Roman Catholic Church. Father Greg had asked me to bring a white veil that he had placed on my head through the Mass. At the end he took it and handed it to me and said now I had to stay as pure as the white veil and I had to bring people to Christ by my example. The day felt like my first birthday—I felt pure, full of joy, and overwhelmed with the presence of God in a special way, and I prayed I could spread this love of Christ. I think I walked on air throughout that day; my happiness was overwhelming.

Now that our marriage was blessed in the Church, I wanted to make sure that all was in order. So, I went before God to pray, and asked, "God, please bless my husband," and paused for the usual question... "Give me a name." But now there was silence. So, I said again, "God bless my husband, watch over him, and guide him." I waited...and there was silence. God never again asked me for a name. He received Simon and me as husband and wife, and we were in a covenantal relationship with God the Father. God had accomplished two things for me through this process. First, I realized that God wanted to participate in my marriage with a blessing. It wasn't distain that He showed me when He asked for the name, but He simply made me realize that He did not recognize that relationship as a marriage.

When we came before Him in the Church and asked for His blessing upon our marriage, and it became a covenant with Him. Secondly, I was affirmed that God hears our prayers! They are so important to Him that He clarifies who we are praying for! How kind and loving was this God, so different than the Allah I had bowed before for forty years and received only silence.

My faith permeated into my life outside the Church and my relationship with Christ deepened. Since most of my friends were Muslims and from Pakistan, I knew that soon I would have to deal with the tough conversation about my conversion. I wanted to honestly inform them since I didn't want to be deceptive—nor did I want to live a lie pretending to be a Muslim. I started to share with a couple of them that I had been having these dreams and visions and I was considering converting to Christianity. They tried to convince me that Islam was the truth and the only way and that this was all my imagination—or they said it was due to Simon's influence. I tried to share from my heart, but they seemed to tune out everything since they were convinced that either my faith was too weak or Simon had brainwashed me. They believed I made up the story as cover up, or perhaps the Devil had possessed me.

I realized that it was futile to keep explaining and defending my husband or my sanity. Eventually, I just informed them that I had converted and was very happy and all was well in my family. They never probed any further, and although they were respectful, I found that I was on the outer fringe of the friendships as I had predicted. I had become an outsider that couldn't be trusted, and I started to feel the change in our friendship, but Jesus was filling me with so much love that I was starting to have the courage to let go.

I continued attending RCIA, and my love for Jesus became deeper and deeper. On Sundays we attended Mass as a family, and I was also attending daily Mass. I longed for Jesus every day, and when I received the Eucharist, I felt peace within me and the strength to go through the work day with its challenges. At this time I was still learning about the Catholic faith, and its teachings about the Eucharist, but as always, my soul was much further ahead than my mind. I was given the gift to understand the truth about the graces that flow from the union with the Body and Blood of Jesus, and my soul would yearn for it every day.

This truth about the power of the Mass was revealed to me by the Devil who couldn't control his hatred for Jesus. One morning I was in bed, thinking about getting up to go to Mass when I heard the evilest, inhuman voice screaming "No!" It sounded like it came from the pits of Hell. It was a blood-chilling shriek that I instantly knew was from Satan, and he was against my decision to go to Mass. At that moment, God allowed me to see and understand the hatred of Satan against the Church and the Mass, which made it clear how important it was for me to attend daily Mass. That morning, I got ready and rushed to church!

God furthered the uncontrollable revelation from Satan about the power of the Mass, and took me deeper into the mystery. He showed me the presence of Jesus at Mass soon after this chilling experience. I had a dream in which I saw a Mass celebrated, and I was one of the few who were able to attend. The Mass began with the priest, but soon he was gone, and Jesus stood in His place and was present until Communion was handed out, at which point the priest became visible again, and Jesus was gone. When I awoke, I was filled with a great joy having attended this Mass with Jesus and the words "Jesus celebrated Mass, Jesus celebrated Mass," on my lips. I was filled with wonder and again that feeling of having been touched in a special way.

When I attended Mass that morning, the wonder was still overwhelming me when I saw Katie, the RCIA director, in the parking lot. The joy was overflowing when I told her about my dream where Jesus celebrated Mass. She smiled at me and said calmly, "But He always celebrates Mass, for during Mass it is Jesus in place of the priest." I didn't realize this was a teaching of the Church, and once again was amazed by how God was continuing to teach and lead me! I was astounded by His love, the way He was showering me with this Grace to build up my faith!

With my devotion to Jesus growing, I felt I needed space in my house that was for Him, so I turned the study into my prayer room, where I spent time every day with Jesus. If I happened to miss a day, I immediately noticed how empty I felt. As I was experiencing this outpouring of Grace, I was rapidly changing.

By now, Simon was going through his own internal struggle. I couldn't believe that my Beloved and I were finally together, that I had finally found the Truth after searching for forty years! I noticed that he seemed irritable, and when I asked him what was wrong, he blamed work or discounted his mood as "Nothing." Little did I know, we were drawing apart.

I was dancing freely now with a new-found abandonment in the arms of my Beloved, my Jesus,—yet little did I know another partner was sitting on the sidelines, someone I loved and who loved me, but how could he ask for a dance? He loved my Beloved as well, and so he watched as I twirled away, oblivious to the storm that was building up.

CHAPTER 15

Lessons in Trust

That Easter, Hamza was received into the Catholic Church as I watched with tears of joy. I knew what graces would flow into his life with Jesus as his Lord. Hamza became very involved in the Teen Life program at the church, and I watched him change into a joy-filled teenager in love with Jesus! The friendships at church challenged him to make good choices and the Sunday night teen meetings helped form his conscience. As a mother, I was delighted to see this change in my son. I had never seen such a joy and a glow on my son's face that was visible now, and it was obvious the source was Jesus. It was another confirmation to me of the fact that a heart that loved Jesus received a joy that the world could not give.

God was teaching me the truths about the faith so fast that at times I struggled to understand what was happening. I was being taught steps to an incredible dance at such a brisk pace that I wondered if I would keep up with it, but it seemed God was confident I could handle it!

One Saturday morning upon waking up, I suddenly felt some type of force or energy enter my body from the crown of my head, and it pulsated through my veins to the tips of my hands and toes. I shook as this liquid fire ran through me, and then suddenly it ended at my toes. I lay there, completely still, petrified! I waited for something else to happen, but everything was suddenly still and normal. I sat up, confused and nervous. What had just happened? I wondered if I looked different as I knew something powerful had happened to me, and I was terrified. Trembling, I walked to the bathroom mirror and peered cautiously at my reflection. I was relieved that I looked and felt completely normal.

Finally, I joined Simon sitting out on the patio, having his coffee. I acted nonchalant, waiting to see if he would notice anything unusual, but he didn't say anything. I made the decision to keep this to myself, unsure how to explain it: dreams, visions, voices, and now this! I paid careful attention to myself in the next few weeks, looking for signs of anything out of the ordinary. Slowly, I started to notice that I now felt an even deeper love for God than ever before. It was a peaceful feeling, a knowledge of the greatness of God and His love for me, and my heart was eagerly responding to this love. Through this deeper love, I became aware of things that were offensive to Him. He showed me thoughts and actions that caused Him pain, and I had a deeper understanding of sin. I received the valuable gift of self-knowledge as if I could hear a gentle voice pointing out areas where I was falling into sin. I was amazed at how differently I was seeing my actions now with this added insight, which revealed my intentions and showed how blind and superficial I had been. I did not like what I was seeing! Basically, I thought I was a good person, always trying to please God and do what was right, but now I witnessed my actions through the lens of God—beneath my actions I saw pride, judgment, anger, resentment, and more darkness. Though it was shocking and unpleasant to see, I was grateful God was revealing this so I could work towards changing and overcoming the sins.

I began the difficult job of internal cleansing—every passing thought I would attempt to hold captive, examine the source and cause, and worked to change my attitude. I realized the many "intruders" or stray thoughts were causing havoc with easy access to my mind, spinning me in many directions. I was receiving guidance and clarity from God regarding what was pleasing to Him and what was displeasing. This helped me tremendously, because I knew what goal I was supposed to move towards, but I knew I had a choice; I could fight against my normal inclination towards selfishness—the easier and comfortable actions--or ignore and turn away from the promptings of God. What I learned from this experience was that God gives us free will and if we decide to turn away, He allows it—and He will allow us to fall and fail. But I also knew He waits for us to turn back, always having a path for us to return. This freedom of choice is God's greatest gift that can also be our biggest problem.

I saw how I had accepted certain things about myself, character traits I didn't consider sins. For example, I would become angry and hurt very quickly, and I felt justified and never examined the actions further. Now God showed me this as a sin, yet I had to look closer to realize why I had these feelings, and how to fight against these emotions.

Another battle I fought against was the viewing of pornography that Tahir insisted become part of our early years of marriage. The images in my mind over the years were vivid, and I was haunted by them. I suffered the torment for as long as they lasted. God asked me to fight against the images when they came, instead of cowering in a corner waiting for them to subside. I started to face them and commanded them to leave—taking authority of my mind, by rebuking them in the name of Jesus. There was no room for them in my mind any longer because I now belonged to Jesus. The most-important lesson God was trying to teach me was to stand in my identity as His daughter and not live in fear. My Father was the King of the Universe, and His eyes were always upon me, and I could trust Him. Overcoming fear has been the hardest battle, and I have come a long way, but this continues to be a promise that the Father continues to remind me of frequently.

As I fought these internal battles, I was surprised by my blindness and the way the Devil manipulated me by feeding me lies, tying me down with fear, and keeping me focused on my pain and wounds. There was a war within my mind and an interior struggle, but on the outside I don't believe anyone noticed. God led me to this internal battle to begin purifying me and strengthening me in the process, and by His grace, I could purge some of the major obstacles that kept me from moving closer to Him.

Today I know that this awakening to and enlightenment about my sins was a result of the fruit from the Baptism of the Holy Spirit, a gift I had received so powerfully that morning when I felt the fire flowing through me. This Grace gave me the ability to see my weaknesses—and through this personal battle, I witnessed firsthand how much Satan hates not only me but each human being who is created in love by God.

As so much was transpiring spiritually within me, I was trying hard to keep things balanced in the physical world. Sania moved away to go to college, and that was a big change for me as I worried about her living on her own and all the things that could go wrong. After all, I was thirty when I lived on my own for the first time, and I was concerned about her having such freedom at her young age. At the same time, I wanted my daughter to be independent and free to make choices. I just prayed hard that she would make the right ones!

I exclusively confided in Simon about what was happening to me. He listened. However, I was totally unaware that he was fighting his own worldy struggles. This spiritual journey was difficult for him to understand. He supported me in my conversion, and he followed me into the Catholic Church. I wanted much more than Sunday

Mass. Our conversations drastically changed. It became difficult for him to understand all the spiritual and mystical things that continued to happen to me, even though he believed they were all real.

God provided someone to help and guide me just as I started to feel frustrated and lonely. Father Rob came into my life, and he turned out to be a blessing. I discovered another gift of the Church, a spiritual director who could help navigate my spiritual life, guide me in my role as a wife and mother, and do it in total confidence. That was exactly what I needed! I recounted to Father Rob the mystical events taking place, and the way Jesus was drawing me into a relationship on a deeper level. I was not satisfied seeing Jesus at daily Mass, or just on Sunday for an hour since I thought about Him constantly—and I felt at times that I was abnormal as my interest in the physical world was declining rapidly. Father Rob helped me keep my balance and build my faith and confidence that I was truly being led by God.

My conversations with my family naturally changed as everything was now filtered through the Bible and my growing relationship with Jesus. One example of this was when Simon, Hamza, and I went to visit Sania. We were having lunch, laughing and talking, and the conversation moved on to the topic of the new friends Sania had made and how things were going.

Suddenly I said very seriously, "We are at war! Make no mistake about it. You need to know that so you can fight. But remember, we are winning!" Everyone looked at me in shock and then began to laugh because I looked so serious. I was a little taken back myself with what had just come out so strongly.

"Yes, Mom, we are at war!" They laughed and indulged me, listening while I explained how serious the battle was for our souls. I became the mother and wife—obsessed with God who had just shifted from Allah to Jesus. On the surface, it may have sounded very similar to the Muslim fear of offending Allah, but in reality, it was completely different. As a Muslim, I had lived in fear of God and followed His laws to avoid Hell, but as a Christian, I followed God and avoided sin out of love for Him. I longed to be with Him forever in Heaven. Because of love, I had recognized the enemy of love and the spiritual warfare that was waged by Satan to tear us away from the loving arms of God the Father. I was in awe at the majesty of God, and because I loved Him for all He had done for me, and His love for me, I wanted to make every effort to please Him. Now it was all about love, not fear.

This love was making me restless, and I wanted to do something for Jesus whom I loved so much! Father Rob was patient, understanding, and explained that all I had to do was receive the Lord's love— I didn't need to earn His love. This concept was foreign; I learned I must earn Allah's forgiveness and mercy to please Him. In contrast, Father Rob taught me about Jesus giving His love and mercy freely—and all He wanted in return was for me to be open to receive. In fact, I knew that He wanted to share this with every person, not just me. I was not special, but His love was, and now that I clearly saw my weaknesses and sins, it amazed me that Jesus didn't hold His love back from me. He truly had come for sinners!

One lesson on discernment that Father Rob taught me has been indispensable for me as it has guided me in the decisions I make. He said, "You are not free to do something unless you are free not to do it. God wants us to be free and that is a great gift He gave us. With God, there is no compulsion, only an invitation. To discern what we are to do in any situation we first have to be free, and only then can we make the right choice."

It was an important lesson for me as I had lived most of my life experiencing no freedom, interior or exterior, and it opened my eyes to see how many places I had operated out of fear and made wrong choices. When I met Jesus, He offered me love and total freedom to choose in every situation. I now wished to model this new freedom in my marriage, family, and work relationships.

Jesus wanted me to be His friend, not a slave. I tried hard just to receive His love, but I continued to feel restless, the extreme love I had for Him was overflowing, and I wanted to thank Him by doing something in return. Living between two worlds that had become equally real, the spiritual and the temporal, sometimes caused confusion and loneliness as most of the world ignored the spiritual. It helped me tremendously to have a confessor who understood this love that consumed me and helped me discern the mysterious ways God was speaking to me. He wisely kept me from getting attached to the experiences.

"It's about the Giver, not the gifts; we should love and serve Him whether He chooses to give us consolations, gifts, or nothing. Our love for Him should not be attached to getting anything, but just loving Him for who He is. That way you will love Him in total freedom."

The mystical events continued to happen in my life, some so precious and special to me that only my confessor could understand and continue to reaffirm that this was indeed from Jesus. This blessing is available to everyone. Jesus's love is so bountiful that He wants to fill every heart that opens itself to Him. He wants a deep personal relationship with each person who is willing to open their own heart to Him, no matter how imperfect. And this truly happened to me one blessed day.

I met Richard, a lonely elderly gentleman at church and developed a friendship with him. Not long after, he became sick and passed away on Easter Sunday of 2010. His funeral Mass was later that week, and I attended my first Catholic funeral. My heart around that time was heavy, having a deep awareness of the sins and blasphemies committed against the Lord.

During the consecration, my heart broke as I considered Jesus and His pain. Almost subconsciously I began consoling Him, praying and offering my heart as a place for Him to rest. I was aware of the brokenness of my heart as I offered it to Him. But my love and compassion won out. I boldly proclaimed, as I got up to receive Communion, "Lord, however, broken and unworthy my heart is, I give it to You with all my love, and invite You to come and rest in it. I will protect You in my undeserving heart, and today I will ask You for nothing!"

I could hardly bear this love I had for Jesus within me! As I made this offering and walked up to receive Communion, I felt my heart open and receive Him. I cried through it, my heart overflowing with the experience of His love and pain. As I drove out of the church parking lot, I knew I carried the Most Holy in my heart, and I took extra care with my thoughts, words, and deeds so as not to disturb Him or cause Him pain.

As this event happened, I did not fully understand what was taking place—it felt like I was on two planes at once, but at the same time I was functioning and fully conscious. I was very aware of His presence as He rested in my heart all day, and I felt like a protective mother who did not want to disturb her resting child! Me, a sinful creature, protecting my God! How could this be? My God, my Lord, how much I love you! That was a Grace-filled day, and though I couldn't understand how this was possible, especially knowing I was unworthy, I couldn't deny His incredible presence and how silent my whole being had become. As I worked that day, I stayed silent as much as possible and had no desire to eat, but rather felt a need to fast.

I was introduced to the army of saints in the Catholic Church one weekend when Simon and I visited a shrine dedicated to Mary. After praying, we went into the beautiful gift shop. It was a huge store filled with statues, rosaries, books, and every religious item one would ever desire. I was near the back of the store approaching the books when a picture on a cover caught my eye. It was the face of a man who appeared to be staring at me. The eyes drew me in, and I felt as if I was supposed to know him, like we were somehow connected. Walking over, I picked up the book, and it was someone I never heard of before —St. Padre Pio of Pietrelcina.

This was the first introduction to the beautiful saints of the Church, and was the beginning of my relationship with this powerful Italian saint. As I read Saint Padre Pio's story over the next few days, I felt connected to him in some mystical way. He became my friend and teacher, and I felt I had someone watching over me. Slowly I began to read the lives of other saints as well, inspired by their examples of holiness. They seemed alive and present, willing to help with their intercession and example to guide me on the right path. I looked at them as a model for my life and longed to have the same heroic virtues. Padre Pio became my dearest friend and soon I got to know many other great saints.

The immense richness of the Catholic faith, and the treasures of its teachings overwhelmed me. I was like a starving person before an unending buffet of rich food and drink. My soul was soaking up and taking its fill of riches of the faith that brought me to a closer union with God. All of the Sacraments offered within the Church continued to work within my soul and my openness to continue to receive instruction and grow in my relationship set the scene for the next amazing event to take place.

The music continued to gently move me closer and closer to my Beloved, whom I could commune with even without words—it was set to a rhythm that was familiar, yet I had never heard it before.

In 2011 Father Rob invited Simon and I on a pilgrimage to the Holy Land. It would be incredible to walk where Jesus had walked, and it would help us understand the Bible better. I was excited about visiting the Holy Land and walking where Jesus walked, but a part of me was also apprehensive about leaving the United States and going back to the Middle East. Since I had come to the United States in 1999, I had never left the country. Now, the thought of leaving brought reminders of past fears, as well as new ones, especially of being stuck in the oppressive culture of the East from where I had escaped. I was trying hard not to let this fear rob me of the joy of the upcoming trip.

To make matters worse, the Arab Spring erupted. It started in December of 2010 in Tunisia, and I watched the revolutionary wave spread from there to Egypt, Libya, Yemen, and many more of the Middle Eastern countries. I knew in my heart that this was the beginning of a very dark period. The news media lauded the citizens for rising to overthrow dictatorships and calling for democracy. I watched in amazement and listened to the ignorance of the "specialists" who believed this violence would give birth to democracy whereas I knew it would become a vacuum for terrorism.

I felt that this was not going to be a "life-bearing spring," but a "death-bearing winter" of the Middle East. It would spread chaos to the entire world. I understood the mindset of the people there, those who were divided by religious factions and tribal mentality—to them that was more important than democracy. To attain peace in this area, a dictator with a show of strength would have to rule— one with complete control over the internal divisions. While this might appear harsh to Western ears, I knew that for democracy to prosper, unity among the people for a greater good was required. The hearts and minds in the Middle East were not at all conducive to this way of thinking.

I shared my fears with Simon that this "Arab Spring," was the beginning of the end of the controlled peace in the Middle East, and I believed that the spark that began this in Tunisia and spread so rapidly was purposely aimed to start chaos and turmoil. The goal was a place for terrorism and violence to prosper. I didn't want to now travel to Israel during this uncertain time! We watched the news closely, and Father Rob contacted the tour company to check on the situation in Israel. The company reassured us that the pilgrimage would get canceled if there was any threat to Israel, and we need not be concerned.

I fervently prayed, desiring to be where Jesus spent His life on earth, but fearful of being stuck in the middle of the conflict. Father Rob with our small group of travelers, and my other friends seemed peaceful and committed to going which encouraged me. Eventually, Simon and I found the peace to say, "Yes," to surrender our fears, and to place our trust in God. Hamza was in his senior year of high school, so my parents graciously came to stay with him. They were understandably stressed about the upcoming trip and not happy at all with our decision. Over the years, they remained silent about the differences in our faith to keep the peace, and when the day finally came for us to leave, they smiled and sent us off and spent the next ten days praying for our safe return.

The flight to Jerusalem was long, but throughout it I experienced an awareness of the difference of this journey to any other. I felt joy, peace, and the presence of God's protection. I didn't feel any of the previous fear and anxiety, and the company of my faith-filled friends and the other pilgrims transformed the trip. I distinctly felt this pilgrimage was anointed.

The time in the Holy Land turned out to be peaceful and filled with many graces at all the beautiful sites. I found the three days that we spent on the Mount of Beatitudes to be the most anointed as I felt Jesus' presence very strongly. The Holy Sepulcher that contains

Calvary and the Tomb of Jesus was where I was overwhelmed with His love, and couldn't hold back tears every time I visited. Simon and I spent the ten days overwhelmed with awe and wonder, finding it hard to believe that we were walking in the steps of Jesus, and we tried to take in everything and memorize it forever. At the end of the ten days, we boarded our flight from Tel Aviv back to the United States, exhausted and sad to be leaving. I was so thankful to God for the opportunity to come on this pilgrimage, and for the friends who had encouraged us to go. We settled in for the long flight home and soon fell asleep. On the flight, I had another prophetic dream.

I was moving from my house to another nearby city. The new house was a simple, two-story home, but my heart was overflowing with joy because of the location. A lady came to visit this new home, and I happily showed her around. We were standing by the staircase, and I was telling her how happy I was because of the location. I couldn't see her face, just her back, but she said some kind things and then left. As I shut the front door, I looked out the window to watch as she walked away. Suddenly she turned around, and her face became grotesque and demonic. She started to say the most horrible obscenities and curses while staring at me, but it was aimed against Jesus. The hatred was so strong that I felt it physically and I stumbled back.

As the demons were hurling these blasphemies, it was all-dark around them, and there was a large group of people-demons that joined her, screaming with her their hatred for Jesus. The scene was so ugly and the words so painful to hear. Since they were all staring at me through the window, I became scared and ran to another window that was on the adjacent side of the house. Opening it, I prepared to jump out and run away. What I saw outside that window stunned me—there was a Eucharistic procession going by, with a priest carrying a Monstrance. Alongside were other priests, Saints, and many people following the procession, singing praises to God. There was light there and a gentle breeze.

I desperately wanted to warn them to run away because around the corner were demons who hated the Lord and would come after them when they heard the singing. Before I could open my mouth, I heard a voice say, "I have drawn a line between My people and the Evil One, and the Evil One cannot cross that line." The fear left me as I knew it was God who had spoken, and I felt a protection and peace descend upon me, and I joined in the procession singing praises to God. I knew the demons were screaming in unimaginable hatred around the corner, but they were held back in their own hell unable to touch us.

I woke up nauseated by the absolute hatred I had physically felt coming against Jesus whom I loved so much. I had experienced the exact opposite of the love that filled my heart for Jesus, and this hate was hard for me to bear. The demonic faces were etched in my memory. I knew this was a dream with a message and wrote it in my journal. Journaling was new to me, but at Father Rob's prompting, I had started to write down certain dreams and experiences. Writing my private and spiritual thoughts did not come naturally for me, and it took discipline and time to become more comfortable with it. I am so thankful that I did this, because otherwise I could not recall or share these events exactly as they happened.

Soon after our return home from the Holy Land, my parents left, and life was back to normal. My son graduated from high school that year and left for college. I had a hard time adjusting to my youngest leaving home. My children were an important part of my life, and from a young age, they were a pivotal part of my identity and purpose. I was accustomed to caring for them, and my life revolved around them. When Hamza left, I felt lost and lonely, and I missed him terribly. I didn't know how to adjust without my children as part of my daily life.

As happens in a marriage sometimes, the gaps in a relationship begin small and then grow wider without noticing. With Hamza gone off to college, I noticed how far Simon and I had drifted apart in our lives. Simon was often traveling for work, and it started to remind me of my life with Tahir.

This was a wake-up call for me. When we first married, I felt secure with the joy, laughter, and family vacations that Simon brought to my life and my children's lives. How could our marriage survive? Through the next few months, I tried to rebuild our relationship as best I knew how. Simon's travels for work increased while I immersed myself in my faith, family, and work commitments.

One day I was doing some housework when I heard God speak again, loud and clear, "Your work here is done, and it's time for you to go." I immediately understood that maybe we were supposed to move. I also knew where we were to move— a nearby the city within a specific area. I had no doubt that it was God speaking because as always there was authority, love, and peace that came with His voice.

I was confused as to why God would ask us to move an hour away from everything that seemed important. Our work, family, friends (my Muslim friends were still in my life though things had become strained), and the church where my conversion took place and which I was attached to, plus I loved our house. So why would He want us to move? As I pondered His words, I was reminded of my dream on the flight back from Israel about moving to this city. I prayed about it, thinking I might be mistaken but the feeling never went away. I thought that maybe this change would help our marriage, and while Simon nonchalantly agreed.

The kids had left, so it was much easier as we didn't have schools to think about. As I continued to pray and think, the feeling persisted that we move. We decided to list our house for sale. If this was not God's will, I thought we would know based on how the process went.

The day the "For Sale" sign was hung in the yard I cried, not wanting to move from the home I loved. Surprisingly though, in a couple of days, I noticed that I became detached from all the things that had seemed so important in the past. I now had peace about the move and knew without a doubt that we had to proceed forward. It's amazing how at times when God asks us for obedience to do things that seem so difficult, when you decide to do it for Him, He gives you the Grace!

By 2012, the housing market had crashed, and it was the worst time for us to sell. When my family and friends heard we were putting our house on the market, they were shocked. I told them we were moving into the city nearby, and they were even more surprised as it would take us farther away from our work. But what could I say? The truth that God had spoken to me about the move would sound silly to them! They already considered my actions outlandish according to their cultural norms: getting divorced, marrying outside the faith and culture, and changing my religion.

To add that I was hearing messages from God would be too strange! I decided to give an answer they could believe: we loved the arts and restaurants in the city, and since children were out of the home, we decided to move closer to downtown. I knew that it sounded frivolous, but that was the best I could come up with and still be truthful. I did love going to the city, and the children were out of the home that allowed for that freedom.

The house showings began and along with that, the frustrations of selling a home. A few months passed and I began to wonder if I had heard God correctly. The offers we received were ridiculously low, and then even those stopped. It was getting close to the holidays, and I was feeling slightly foolish.

I began feeling that God was calling me to spend time alone with Him. The word "retreat" kept coming up in prayer, though I had never been on a retreat and wasn't sure how it was done. It was

November, and Simon was going out of town again, so he suggested I go on the retreat at the same time.

I was nervous and scared as I knew that God wanted me alone and quiet. The thought of spending four or five days with no television, phone calls, and only God and me was frightening! Simon didn't understand my hesitancy since I loved God and here was a chance to spend days with Him uninterrupted!

I couldn't explain why I was scared to be alone with God, the one whom I talked about continuously, but Simon encouraged me to go so I booked a private five-day retreat.

My Beloved spoke to me and said to me, "Arise, my darling, my beautiful one, come with me."

– Song of Solomon 2:10

CHAPTER 16

The Retreat

On that November morning, Simon left for his trip, and I drove to the church for Mass before the retreat. I felt nervous as I sat through the Mass and asked God to be with me and guide me. Afterward, I went to the church narthex before heading out to pick up a bulletin. It was there I felt Jesus's presence very strongly! He told me not to be afraid, that He would walk with me and I would not be alone. As I walked to the car, I was acutely aware of Him walking with me, and I felt peace.

The retreat house was on a beautiful lake, and my cottage was next to the chapel. It was a gorgeous sunny day, and I unpacked and took a walk alongside the lake. Later in the afternoon, I met with Father Jonathan who was the spiritual director at the retreat house. I briefly shared my conversion story with him and how I felt God had called me to spend time with Him, which was why I was there. He gave me a folder with some information on retreat guidelines, and daily scripture verses that I could pray. He asked me to start with the first one that night, and we would meet the next day for discussion.

I had also brought a book with me by Father Gaitley, entitled *Consoling the Heart of Jesus, A Do-it-Yourself Retreat.* The title had seemed perfect, and I thought it would be a good guide for my first retreat. So after meeting Fr. Jonathan, I started the book. The idea of consoling and offering myself to Jesus resonated, as it reminded me of Richard's funeral when I had offered Jesus my heart, and He had truly come and rested.

I entered the dining hall for dinner that evening, and I was surprised to see it full of priests. It turned out that there was a retreat for priests that had started that day as well, so being the only woman and a Muslim convert, I was feeling a bit uncomfortable. I went to a corner table with my book and food and tried to keep true to the intention of a silent retreat. As I walked back to my cottage that evening, I savored the beauty of the flowers, the trees, the serene lake, and I breathed in the silence and peace. It seemed that Nature was singing a melody that was filling my heart. As the sun went down, I sat in the rocking chair outside my room looking out on the lake as my mind slowly started to settle down and let go of the distractions and let go of thoughts about my daily life.

When the sun finally set and the beautiful colors in the sky turned dark, it became really quiet, and I realized there was no one in any of the cottages on this side of the lake. Suddenly I felt nervous and a little scared, but looking across to my right I saw the chapel, and in the window, I could see the Tabernacle with the light burning there, and I felt better that Jesus was close. I went into my cottage, and it was 7:30. With no distractions of TV, phone, family, or chores, I was settled in bed by 8:00. I opened the folder and read the directions on *Lectio Divina* (meditating on Scripture), and I settled back to read the first assigned Scripture. What transpired afterward I am sharing from my journal entry to preserve the authenticity, and also because I don't think I could recapture the beauty of what took place.

November 16
Retreat

Matthew 22, The Parable of The Wedding Feast.

Jesus again in reply spoke to them in parables, saying, "The Kingdom of Heaven may be likened to a king who gave a wedding feast for His son. He dispatched his servants to summon guests to the feast, but they refused to come..."

As I read the first two lines about the King, who was having the wedding feast, I found myself at the scene and could see it happening right before my eyes. I could clearly hear the music playing and the voices of people there. I felt as if my soul left, transported there, leaving my body behind, writing and watching.

(I felt led to start writing this down as the vision came.)

All of Heaven is decorated and celebrating. Everything is prepared for the wedding feast. Lights, music, laughter, joy, what splendor! The Bridegroom is ready. He is beautiful, shining, happy, joyful, laughing, waiting—how handsome and larger than life He is! How can this be for me? As much as He is Light, I am dark. His clothes are shining, and I am covered with a dark shawl. I am at the gates and hear the music, and see the lights. I cover my face with the shawl. How can I be the bride?

I am ashamed; everyone will laugh at me, seeing the ugliness and darkness. Look at the incredible beauty of the bridegroom. He was radiant! Look at His house, how magnificent! And look at the bride, totally dark compared to His light! I stood at the gates, cowering in the dark corner, scared, ashamed, and nervous and feeling completely unworthy to be the bride. Unworthy to even be a guest! I look at the bridegroom through the gates... Oh, how I love Him—there is none other like Him. I watch Him from the gates as He is laughing, greeting, and celebrating. I am the bride He is waiting for—but how can I be the bride?

How could He have chosen me?

How I have yearned for Him, longed to be with Him! Oh, desire of all desires, I can't even walk towards you! I want to fly to you, but the contrast between us holds me back. Your love is infinite; my love is finite. I could never give you enough in return. Though I long to love You to the point of dying, it could never be like Your love. So how could I be Your bride? I would fail You. They would all laugh at Your choice. I can't bear to embarrass You. Oh, love of my life, what should I do?

The vision ended there, and suddenly I felt exhausted and unable even to process what had happened, and I fell into a deep sleep. The next morning I woke up, confused about the experience at the wedding feast the night before. Was I really there? Did I make it up? The memory was clear and I felt that I had been physically present and experienced it in person. I recalled the strong emotions in detail, and I knew that it was not my imagination.

I didn't understand the meaning of this vision, so I turned back to reading my retreat book and praying in the chapel. Jesus showed me that day that no relationships would blossom and bear life unless it went through Him. If I started a relationship without Him, it would not bear good fruit, but wither and die. A relationship with Him includes having Him in the center of every other relationship—and then life will flow from Him into every relationship. He is the Life!

I met Father Jonathan for our daily meeting and I shared what transpired the night before. He listened quietly, and he suggested I stay with that scripture that day instead of going to the next lesson. He suggested I go back and interview the guests at the feast. I told him I would try, but I didn't know how I could make the vision come back. I had merely been an observer.

I went to the chapel in the afternoon and was just finishing the Rosary when I was again transported to the wedding feast. It all happened with no effort from me, just the same as the previous evening. I could hear the singing, see the dancing, and see myself standing at the gates, feeling all the same emotions of shame and unworthiness. It had picked up exactly where it had left off!

November 17
In the Chapel

"I stand at the gates in the shadows, watching the celebration. Everyone is joyous. Suddenly Mary is standing by my side, and with her is Mary Magdalen.

She says, "There you are! Hurry up, let's get you dressed."

How can this mother accept me with such love? It's as if she doesn't see my unworthiness, darkness, ugliness, plainess compared to her Son!

"How can you accept me?" I ask her.

"Because my Son accepted you first. He loves you."

I look at Mary Magdalen and ask her, "How are you so filled with joy? Don't you carry the burdens from the past?"

They both exchange looks and smile at each other, and the Virgin Mary, says, "Come with me."

They take me inside the gate to a small cottage that is in the back away from all the festivities. They sit me down inside.

Mary Magdalen looks at me gently and says, "I too was like you. Then one day I heard about the Messiah and being so fed up and tired of my life, I went to see what the crowds were talking about. Who was this miracle worker? That day changed my life. I heard Him preach. His Voice was different from any voice I had ever heard. For the first time, I heard love in a voice. I stood at the edge of the crowd, frozen for what seemed like an eternity. The Light came into my dark life that day. I was able to see for the first time why I was so tired and fed up with my life. Everything came into focus. Through His voice, the chains started to fall away. I could NEVER go back to that darkness. I had seen Light! I just stood there for a long time as if in a trance, seeing my life for the first time in the light. I was overwhelmed and went searching for my Master. I found Him having dinner at a house. In a daze, I pushed my way in, only wanting to fall at His feet. When I came before Him, I fell to my knees and wept at His feet. I wanted to rip my heart out and lay it at His feet, but He lifted me up. He gave me dignity that I never had. I saw the Truth. He was the Savior, and He gave ME dignity! I RECEIVED it, and my heart was filled with joy. Since that day, nothing of the world has touched that joy. You too have to RECEIVE the dignity, the love, and forgiveness too. It is a gift from your Father. Will you refuse Him?"

With this question, the vision ended, and I was back in the chapel holding my rosary. I was amazed at what had just happened. I had heard their words and felt their emotions as well! I knew this was special grace, but I realized that I was to stay passive and allow the Lord to lead me. This was all from Him, and there was nothing I could do to make it happen or control it.

November 17
At Night in the Room

Mary Magdalen says, "Let me go and get Peter. He is the closest to the Lord; he will talk to her." Peter walks in, seeming really busy and out of breath.

"What is going on Mother?" He asks Mary. Then He looks at me confused and says, "Why aren't you ready?"

I think to myself, "He already knows I am the bride, and he is not shocked or repulsed!"

Mary tells him that I don't feel worthy and Peter starts to laugh, "Worthy? Look at me! You think I was worthy? He doesn't care what we are or what we have done. He only wants to know if we love Him. He asked me three times, "Peter do you love me?" That is the most important question. All you have to say is, "Yes Lord, I love you," and He does the rest. His love will transform you; it will make you worthy. Just be happy to receive the gift. Say, "Yes Lord, I love you."

After that advice from Peter, I was back in my room and the vision ended. The next morning, I attended Mass as usual. Arriving early, I sat before the Blessed Sacrament, adoring Jesus. I was amazed at what was being shown to me in this incredible continuous vision! Suddenly, I was back with Peter and the story picked up in the same spot it had ended. Every time it picked up, my emotions were exactly where they left off previously! My feeling and emotions had no trouble entering the vision as if they had never been interrupted.

There I was sitting in the simple cottage with Mary, Mary Magdalen, and Peter urging me to accept the gift I was being given.

November 18
Before Mass, in front of the Blessed Sacrament

Jesus walked in, a radiance flowing from Him, and I shrank to the back of the room. I wanted to disappear, feeling ashamed and embarrassed because I knew He could see everything about me. He was SO beautiful!

Mary spoke up, "She feels unworthy of you."

He smiled and asked everyone to leave. I began to shake. He extended His hand to me and called me by my name. I came before Him, feeling unworthy and small. I knelt before Him. He took my hand in His and gently asked, "Naylah, do you love me?"

As I heard Him, I could feel how much He desired my "yes." Tears began to stream down my face, and I said, "Yes, Lord, I love you!" And as I said it, I felt the word "love" was too small to describe my feeling for my Lord. He smiled, so happy with my answer, and pulled me to my feet. My love seemed so small before His great love that flowed out of Him!

I was back in the chapel before the Blessed Sacrament, tears running down my face. It was time to go into Mass.

I came back to the retreat house after Mass, and as I was walking toward the cottage, I kept hearing that question, "Naylah, do you love me?" It seemed that the trees, the sky, the birds were all in unison, repeating that same question. I went to the chapel and fell on my knees, and I understood the depth of that question. The love He was talking about is not the love that we as humans understand. His Love is the Way of the Cross. My heart cried "yes," but could I be faithful to that "yes"? My smallness was before me, and I knew the Lord saw it all, but He continued to ask that same question, "Naylah, do you LOVE me?" and the emphasis was on the word "love."

I shared the vision with Father Jonathan as it transpired each day, and he instructed me not to resist, and to carefully record the events since he felt the Lord was leading and directing me. When we met daily, Father listened and then prayed with me, and continued to encourage my journaling the events.

November 18
After Lunch

My Jesus, how have I lived all this time without knowing you? Your touch has started a fire deep in my heart, and I burn in it. Oh, what sweetness there is in that burning, that I would die without it! My heart desires to be engulfed in its flames, to be consumed by it!

The vision returns:

I am standing before Jesus with my hand in His, and He asks me the same question a second time, "Naylah, do you love me?"

I look at His gentle face, and I forget my smallness, I just see how much He desires my "yes."

"Yes, Lord, I love you" putting everything I can into that "yes."

He smiles. He is so happy!

He held me to His Heart and asked again, "Naylah, do you love me?"

Feeling the love coming from his Heart, the peace of resting on his Heart, I speak up even louder with more feeling, "Yes, Lord, I LOVE you!"

As I was saying each "yes," I could see His sacrificial love. I was giving Him my broken love, and as I rested on His Sacred Heart, I asked Him to allow me to console His Bleeding Heart through this union of love.

November 18 | 4:15 PM
In the Room

I hear the Lord say it is time to continue…

I find myself in His Sacred Heart again, and the peace is unbelievable. My soul feels rested.

I hear Him say, "I have let you look into my Heart so you can see and know that there is only mercy and love within. Do you understand that there is nothing of which to be afraid? There is nothing, no sin, my Mercy can't wash away."

I feel peace—I have nothing to worry or be ashamed about. His love makes me worthy. I smile at Him. I am ready.

He smiles and takes away my dark shawl and covers me with a white, sparkling cape. I can walk with Him now; I have nothing to fear!

I now understand the joy of all the guests who are dancing and celebrating. I could feel their joy in my heart and my heart leaped with theirs. They have all accepted His unconditional love. They are rejoicing in their freedom and now mine, another sinner who has been saved! They are celebrating my salvation!

I know, Lord, that my love needs to be purified and strengthened, but today I know it is enough for me to be Your bride, to walk with you to Our Father's House. I look in your eyes, and I can see the love You have for me, and it is enough, Lord. I am ready to walk with You!

November 19 | 7:11 AM
Before Mass, in front of the Blessed Sacrament

I was the bride walking with Jesus, my Bridegroom, to the Father's House. Everyone is singing and dancing, celebrating as we walk up to the House. As we get closer, I am nervous. I was going to meet the Father! At the door of the House, Mary greets me, smiling reassuringly. I could feel her telling me in her smile, "If only you knew the love of the Father you would not be nervous."

With Jesus on one side and Mary on the other I walk into the House. It is a living room and God the Father is there, He is the most kind-looking older man with gray hair and a beard. He is telling someone how to put things in order. He looks up and sees me, giving me the most-gentle and love-filled look. The love draws me in like a magnet, and I run to Him crying, "Abba, Father! Oh, how long I have waited for You!"

As I am running, I am a child of about six years old, and as Abba opens His arms to me I can see that He too has waited a long time for me!

"My little one!" He cries, as I run into His arms. He picks me up, and I am enveloped in His arms, and I cling to His neck. Oh, what peace! I am safe! I am home! I am crying with my face buried in His neck. Finally, I peek from His arms, and I see Jesus and the joy on His face, and Mary smiling beside Him.

"I sent my Son to find you and bring you back to me. I missed you, my little one," Abba says. I knew how deeply He meant the words. What a personal relationship this was!

I push closer into my Father's arms and breathed in deeply. I never want to leave!

I spend time snuggled with Abba, and then He asks me to go and spend time with Jesus. I reluctantly come out of the softness and security of His arms and shower his face with kisses before I get down and take Jesus's hand. We walk together for a while.

"Where is the feast?" I ask.

"The Feast is the Union with the Father. That is the destination."

Suddenly, I realized that I would be leaving tomorrow. My heart starts to shake, and I want to weep. I cling to the Lord and bury myself in His Heart. "No, no, no! I don't want to leave." That is all I can say, over and over again.

He holds me close, gently, and lets me rest on His Heart, and I keep crying.

November 19
After Mass

I'm clinging to the Lord, begging Him, "I don't want to leave, Lord. Please don't send me away!"

"We will spend the day just being together. Be at peace."

I love Him SO much; I can't find words...

He holds me close, and I return to the cottage, and we walk by the water together.

I look up at Him every so often, fearful that He might leave. "Lord, my heart is weak; it cannot live away from you!"

10:37 AM
In the Room

"You have seen My love and mercy; you see the peace it brings you. How many don't know the depths of My mercy, and that I wait for them, waiting for them to come to Me, so I can forgive them and give them a new life."

There is a deep sorrow in His voice. "Will you help Me take this love to them? Help them to know Me?"

I feel selfish, clinging to Him and not wanting to let go. I sensed his sadness. "Yes, I will help you, Lord," looking at His sad face with my heart overflowing with love for Him.

"Will you let Me live in You?"

I start to feel hope; maybe Jesus will never be separated from me..."Yes, Lord."

"Will you be my vessel?"

I feel Mary squeeze my hand encouragingly, "Yes, Lord."

He looks relieved and happy and smiles at me with even more love. The pain and panic of separation begins to ease.

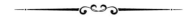

November 20 | 8:50 AM
Feast of Christ the King, Last Day

I am sitting outside my cottage in the rocking chair and feel the presence of Jesus. I thank Him for all the gifts He has given me on this retreat.

> "I will miss you, Lord."
> "I will always be with you."
> "Will I be saying goodbye to the Father?" I ask him.
> Suddenly I feel the breeze blow gently, and the sun's warmth kiss my face, and I feel Abba's presence and love. He is in the air I breathe, in the sunlight on my face, in the breeze, in the waves of the ocean, in the trees, birds, the moon, and the stars. There is no goodbye to the great I Am because He is always present! I was filled with peace and joy, and all sadness leaves me.

I left the retreat to go home filled with peace and happiness, knowing that Jesus would always be with me.

I walked with my Beloved to the Father's house, my heart dancing with all the guests to the beat of the heavenly music.

CHAPTER 17

Coming Down from the Mountain

I returned home a little dazed after this incredible experience that I was still struggling to understand. I had experienced God's love and presence in such an intimate way that it was difficult to adjust to normal life once again. The mystical events were so difficult to explain, but Simon listened as I told him what had transpired.

I also shared this experience with Father Rob who said that it was a great blessing, and I should thank God. He reminded me to continue to journal. He said such spiritual experiences can sometimes become the focus instead of God. So to avoid falling into pride and to stay humble, it was prudent that I should thank God and continue with my daily life as normally as possible. I followed his advice and was once again grateful for his wisdom and insight.

Simon and I finally received an offer on our house and started to look for a place in the city. By now Sania had graduated from college and had begun her first job, and Hamza was in his final year of college. We decided to downsize and settled on a townhouse. We had two months to close and started to pack up the house. I felt excited as this seemed like it was the start of a new life for us.

In the middle of this busy time, Uncle Aslam and Aunty Naseem's youngest son, Faiz was getting married. It was expected to be an elaborate affair—with most of the family coming to the wedding. There was a flurry of preparation and excitement as traditional clothes were ordered and jewelry matched. My parents, sisters, and their families came and stayed with us. The wedding was a weeklong celebration filled with traditional music, dancing, and singing. We stayed at the hotel where the wedding was to take place and invited Maji to stay with us as well. Maji was ninety-five, and though frail, she enjoyed all of the festivities thus far, including the henna ceremony the night before, and was looking forward to her grandson's wedding.

On the morning of the wedding, we all got together for breakfast in Maji's room, including my parents and my sister and her family. By the time Simon and I arrived in the room, everyone was already there, and an excited discussion was underway. Maji's face was glowing, and she had a look of wonder and awe as she insisted that my mother go outside and look for someone. Hamza was sitting on a chair with a dazed look. I asked what had happened, and Maji turned to me and said, "They were all just here, He was just here! Go out and look in the hallway. They must still be there!"

"Who was here?" I asked, beginning to get concerned.

She said, "I told them—the one they pray to in the church. He was here—and everyone was worshipping Him, and I too joined them and worshiped Him. It was beautiful! We just knelt and worshiped Him in silence; we didn't utter a word!"

My mother said, "Maji, who was it? Are you talking about Jesus?"

"Yes, Him! He was here, I'm telling you, just go out, and you will see the whole procession! You just missed it!" she exclaimed.

I was speechless. My sister whispered to me that Maji had just woken up, and she kept saying the same thing over and over again. I noticed my son Hamza, sitting there stunned as if he had been hit by a ton of bricks. I sat by him, and asked if he was OK. "Yes, I just can't believe it."

"I know," I said, "it's amazing."

"No," he explained, "you don't understand. Last night on the way back from the party I was sitting next to Maji, and I wished that she would know Jesus. I just prayed, 'Jesus, I wish you would reveal yourself to her so she would know you,' and last night He came to her!"

I stared at my son, speechless! Jesus had heard Hamza's heartfelt, loving prayer, and immediately answered it! I was delighted by the confirmation of faith my son received, as well as the blessing for my dear grandmother who was so special to me. What a gift she had been given!

We had to get ready for the wedding, and I didn't get a chance to discuss it further. But that night, when I was alone with Maji as she lay in bed with a wistful smile on her face, and a far-away look in her eyes, she asked me, "Do you think He will come again tonight?"

"I don't know Maji; I hope He does."

I don't know if Maji had any other dreams after that as she never mentioned it again, and six months later she passed away. I believe that she accepted Jesus that night when she chose to worship and adore Him. Jesus had gently led my beloved, Maji in the last dance of her life, bringing her safely home.

As the music drew to a close for Maji, she suddenly found herself in the arms of her Beloved, who gently led her off the dance floor to the Father's house.

After Faiz's wedding we got busy with our move. The detachment from the house stayed consistent, and when we handed over the keys, Simon and I were both looking forward to a new life in the city. The next few months were spent settling into our townhouse. Adjusting to a smaller space was challenging, and for me, the hardest compromise was a tiny kitchen in comparison to our previous house. We added cabinets and storage in the garage, and became settled.

We attended a well-known Catholic church in the area and began building relationships in a new community. I discovered that there were four Catholic churches close by which allowed us to have many options depending on the time of services. I found one church close to us that had morning Mass at a time convenient for me before work, and I started attending daily Mass. I was drawn to its simplicity. It was a Franciscan parish, and I felt like I was home. We decided to make St. Patrick's Church our parish.

Shortly after we settled into our townhouse, we found some problems in the construction that would require a substantial amount of money to fix. We had taken a loss when we sold our house, and the move had stretched us financially. Now with this issue, we were looking at another big expense. Simon became stressed with some other changes happening at work, and this just added to the problems.

We tried to stay positive about the move, but things didn't get better, and only continued to get more complicated. Doubts started to creep into my mind, and guilt began to weigh me down. This move had all been because of me; I had heard God ask us to move, and now we were in a mess! Though Simon remained quiet, distant, and stressed, I continued to feel worse every passing day.

One day it really weighed on me as I was driving home. I was lost in thought about the issues with the house that kept piling up, and I wondered if I had been wrong about the move. Maybe God had not spoken to me about moving. Maybe it had just been my mind, and I had made a big mistake! That is when I heard God speak to me internally with these words. They were clear and in direct answer to my fears.

"How do you think you got here? Was it not My voice that led you? So why do you doubt My voice now?" As I heard these words I was reminded of my search for Truth, how I had found it, and how He had spoken to me—and most especially the retreat! I was reminded of all the amazing things that had happened, and the fact that it had been His voice that had led me, and how I had followed Him in taking the biggest leap of faith: leaving Islam for Christianity!

I was stunned and speechless after hearing those words. What could I say? God was right; it had been His voice that had led me and I had taken the hardest step of following His voice to step out in faith. Really, how could I doubt Him now? I apologized to God for doubting Him and said I would trust Him with this next step. After that incredible conversation with God on my drive home, I was convinced again that it had been God's will for us to move.

The financial concerns still weighed upon my heart, though I had accepted God had truly called us to move. A few days later I was coming down the stairs in the house, the worry about the expenses heavy, when again I heard Him speak to answer my fears. Internally I heard these words, "Do you not think I am your Father? Don't you trust that I will give you everything you need and when you need it? You give your children an allowance, not your whole bank account, because that would not be good for them. But you want Me to give you the control of the bank account, because you don't think I, your Father, will give you your allowance? Do you trust yourself more than Me?"

Again, I was being given a deeper understanding of the words I was hearing. If God gave me everything at once, I would be incapable of managing it correctly, and I would make mistakes. Because God the Father loved me, He gave me a controlled allowance so I would not make mistakes that would cause me harm. I felt His deep love for me as He spoke these words, and I realized how much He longed for me to trust Him. Tears ran down my face as I felt His love and I told Him that I trusted Him better than myself, and peace filled my heart and all worry and doubt regarding our finances also left. Shortly after these reassurances from God, all the issues got resolved with a minimal cost, and finally Simon and I could enjoy the new city.

The following year we had an opportunity to go to Medjugorje, a place I had a deep desire to visit since I had first heard of it. Our pilgrimage to Medjugorje was different from the Holy Land, as there weren't as many places to see. More time was allotted for prayer and reflection, and I felt a deep peace in this tiny town in former Yugoslavia. Surrounded by thousands of people who loved the Lord and shared the faith, I felt a deep sense of community which was centered on the Lord. Walking through vineyards to the famous St. James Church, we passed people saying the Rosary and praying with no reservations, and soon we were doing the same. Praise and worship happened openly and spontaneously throughout the town; here it was all about Jesus!

Thousands of pilgrims attended the outdoor Adoration, and the Monstrance was huge! It was another wonderful experience of Heaven on earth, where we could worship with others who loved and adored the Lord! I also discovered while there that the Blessed Mother had requested two days for fasting for the reconciliation of sinners. These days were on Wednesdays and Fridays. I was already fasting on the same two days, not because I knew this from an understanding of Medjugorje, but because I had felt called by Mary to do this soon after my conversion! Once again it was a reaffirmation that I had been led on this faith-journey totally by the hands of the Lord through Mary's intercession.

Throughout the pilgrimage, wherever we went, I noticed there were statues or pictures of Padre Pio, including at the guesthouse where we were staying. I felt happy to see him and felt that he was on the pilgrimage with me in a special way. I felt Mary urge me to buy a miraculous medal; it was a strong feeling, but because I didn't know much about the miraculous medal or know about the devotion tied to wearing medals, I didn't pay attention to this prompting. After the pilgrimage ended, Simon and I took a few extra days to spend in Croatia along the beautiful Adriatic coast. As we spent time in breathtakingly beautiful Dubrovnik and wandered through the old city, I remembered the prompting to buy a miraculous medal, and I terribly regretted that I had not bought it in Medjugorje. On one of those days, we went to a Franciscan monastery and spent some time praying. I noticed the statues of different saints, and I felt sad that I didn't see an image of Padre Pio. I said in my heart, *Padre Pio I miss you. You were with me through the pilgrimage, but now I don't see you.* I missed his presence!

That night, when we got to the hotel, we decided to watch a movie. We got comfortable, and stretched our tired legs, worn out from walking all day. I opened Simon's backpack to get the fresh figs I had bought earlier. As I pulled the bag out, I noticed something shiny at the bottom of the backpack. I put my hand in, expecting a coin that may have fallen, but instead I pulled out a small safety pin with two medals on it; a miraculous medal and a Padre Pio medal! My mouth was dry as I looked at them in stunned silence! They were old looking, and the Padre Pio medal looked like it could have held a relic. I turned to Simon, holding the pin up with the medals hanging from it.

"What is it?" he asked noticing the look on my face.

"They are medals," I finally said, "did you put these in the bag?"

"I have never seen them before, and they weren't in the bag this morning. I empty the backpack and refill it daily, and I know those were not in there this morning," he said, as I handed him the medals with a stunned look.

I told him about the prompting in Medjugorje to buy the miraculous medal and missing Padre Pio's image at the Franciscan monastery. Simon looked shocked as he heard this, and we both stared at the medals, unable to explain it— especially amazed at them appearing on a pin together! This was a special gift that I brought back with me from Medjugorje, and a new appreciation of the blessings from medals worn in faith.

What a peaceful dance this had become, the melody soothing and the steps slow and gentle, as my Beloved laid gifts before me, encouraging me to trust His lead.

CHAPTER 18

The Final Dance

A year went by, and I had settled into our new life in the city. St. Patrick's parish had been a good fit, and I had started volunteering there as a Eucharistic Minister for the homebound. The Eucharist was the center of my faith, and I longed for that communion with Jesus daily. I wanted to help in bringing Jesus to those who longed for Him and were unable to attend Church.

Hamza graduated college and got a good job, and I felt relieved that now I had accomplished what I had set out to do. Both my children had freedom and education, the two things I had promised myself years ago when I left the Middle East. In addition to this, they also had come to know Jesus, who was the Way, the Truth, and the Life. I was so thankful! America had truly turned out to be a city shining upon a hill and had bestowed on me more gifts than I could count.

Seven years had passed since my conversion when the word "charismatic" suddenly came to mind, and while I had heard it mentioned some time ago, I didn't know much about it. Yet it

repeatedly kept coming to my thoughts with an additional word—
Charismatic retreat! I looked it up and read about the renewal of the
Baptism of the Holy Spirit explained as a new Pentecost. I had
personally experienced a rebirth when the fire of the Holy Spirit had
come upon me bringing with it a deep understanding of God's love
and the separation from God that sin creates. I knew that without the
Holy Spirit, we operated only with our human understanding, but
with the Holy Spirit, we received God's wisdom and power that
empowered us to go beyond our human capabilities.

Since I was drawn to its core teaching, the feeling to attend a
Charismatic retreat only grew stronger. I started to look for something
in the area. Immediately one retreat popped up that was a two-hour
drive, taking place in a couple of weeks. I searched for more, but only
found one. The time worked for me, and by now Simon was
accustomed to me relating what I felt God wanted from me. He told
me I should book the retreat.

I mentioned it to my friend Maria, who smiled saying she too
had the same prompting and had just booked that retreat! Three weeks
later, Maria and I walked in late to the annual Charismatic retreat, and
the first speaker had already started. Jesse Romero, a well-known
Catholic evangelist, was speaking about Islam and how it was different
from Christianity. He spoke powerfully, and it was obvious that he
had a good understanding of Islam and its teaching. I listened to him,
amazed at how well he explained the rise of violence. At the first break,
I introduced myself to him and explained how impressed I was with
his knowledge, and thanked him for speaking the truth. I told him I
understood it well as I was a convert from Islam and had been a
Catholic now for seven years. When he heard how Jesus brought me to
the Catholic Church, he insisted that in his second talk he wanted to
invite me to share the words that Jesus had spoken from the Cross to
me. He said people needed to hear that Jesus was working miracles
even today, and their hope and faith needed to be built up.

I looked around at the large group of about 500 people and turned pale. I couldn't imagine standing in front of so many people and speaking, but at the same time, how could I not tell everyone how amazing Jesus is and that He is alive and with us! I nervously nodded, and Jesse Romero smiled and told me just to say what I had told him.

The next day Jesse called me up to share my testimony. I stood before the people, opened my mouth, and felt that I was lifted up from the ground. As I spoke about what Jesus did for me, I felt power go through me, and a peace rest over me. This was what He wanted me to do. I knew it like I had never known anything before. When I came down from the stage, people came and hugged me throughout the day until the end of the retreat. I was told how much my testimony had impacted their faith. I knew then that I had to tell others what Jesus had done in my life. I had to share my testimony to remind people that Jesus was not just a historical figure, but a living Lord who was still working miracles. I had to share the gifts I had received for He wanted to pour out His love on all people! He was asking for us to trust Him who can do all things, even spin a devout Muslim like me completely around, and all for the sake of His love.

I returned home with a new desire to proclaim the love of Jesus, and I also knew that I had to write a book so that He could be glorified. On my return, things started to move quickly. Jesse contacted me to do a radio interview with him, and soon the pastor at St. Patrick's asked me if I would share my story with the staff and then the parish. This was the beginning of a new mission Jesus gave me, and soon I was having multiple radio interviews and started speaking at different Catholic groups and churches. Every time I stood up to share my testimony, I felt God's love, and peace, and my heart was filled with joy. He had done so much for me—the least I could do was tell everyone about Him! I felt like the leper who had been healed and wanted to thank Him, and I wanted everyone to know about Him and His love (Luke 17:11-19).

My family had accepted my conversion, and realized that it was not a passing fancy. Most of my Muslim friends had moved on, and the friendships had faded away, and in their place, I now had some deeply, faith-filled Catholic friends who truly loved me. I felt like Mary was making a rosary for me, and each of my new friends was a pearl she handpicked and was threading into this fabric of my life. They had come into my life as true gifts, and the purity of love that I felt from them was something I had never experienced in any of my previous friendships. It was Christ in the center who was giving life to our friendship. It was in this gesture of friendship and love that I signed up for my first women's retreat.

It was organized by the Magnificat women's group led by two holy nuns from a Charismatic order, and held at the same place where I had gone for my private retreat some years ago and had the profound experience with the Lord. The first night of the retreat was the introduction with time for praise and worship, and then we had time to pray. Strangely, that night my heart felt heavy, and all the painful memories of my life seemed to be rising to the surface. I felt mentally and emotionally tired, and I just wanted to be alone.

I was only half listening and wishing I could leave, as Sister Cecilia was speaking. It was then that I felt the Lord say to me, "I will show you your life flowing under My eyes. All is connected—it is not in pieces. That is how you see it, but I will show you through My eyes."

It was strong enough that I scribbled this down even as I felt sorry for myself, and at the same time, I wasn't sure it was a word from the Lord. I had always struggled with doubting myself since I had not been affirmed most of my life. God had demonstrated to me over time that it was Him. Yet I always fell into Satan's trap of not trusting that it was indeed God's voice.

With doubt, sadness, and frustration, I decided to go to the chapel to be alone and pray instead of joining my friends to socialize. I wanted time to complain to the Lord! As I knelt before the Tabernacle, I saw an interior image of myself exhausted and weary of life, sitting on the ground leaning against a wall. I didn't have any energy to get up; I was tired of my journey. I physically felt the exhaustion as I knelt before the Tabernacle.

Suddenly, in this interior vision, I saw Jesus standing before me, His hand stretched out to me. I put my hand in His, and He pulled me up and started to dance with me. I am not a great dancer, but at this moment, I was dancing perfectly! Jesus was twirling me around, and my hair flew in the air as I was spinning and laughing with exuberant joy. It was the delight of just being together! Amazingly, there was no music, but there was an incredible harmony as we danced. I felt the strength of His hand on my back as He held me, and I realized that I would not make any mistakes or stumble because He was leading the dance! He would not let me miss a step! I could barely contain the joy, and I felt so safe and protected! I didn't need any music because with Jesus I had the perfect melody and the perfect Partner! This was the final and ultimate dance in the arms of my Savior, my best dance, executed perfectly and requiring no music. I felt all the movements as I danced, my body moving most gracefully as it surrendered itself to the Lord. The joy we shared is difficult to put into words; it was beyond any feeling of happiness I had ever experienced, and it stemmed from the fact that all things were in order in His presence. Nothing could go wrong; there was no fear, doubt, worry or questions. It just was a pure and holy joy.

Then the Lord spoke: "My daughter, walk with me through your life."

As I heard this, I started writing. I heard the Gospel of John:
"In the beginning was the Word
The Word was with God; the Word was God
He was in the beginning with God.
All things came to be through Him, and without Him,

nothing came to be.
What came to be through Him was life
And this life was the Light of the human race.
The Light shines in the darkness
And the darkness has not overcome it.

Then the Lord continued:

"Through me, you came to be. I asked if you would go into the world and do My work. I showed you that it would be difficult and painful, but I would always be with you. I chose the home you were to be born in, and I showed you all of it. You said "yes", you would enter into the world and be My hands and feet; you would have My heart and My words. So, My child, through Me you came to be in your mother's womb. I was with you. You spent nine months awaiting your birth. Then the day came for your birth, and you entered a broken world. The world you had promised to help Me save. Your cries at birth were drowned out by the wails and lamentations of this bruised and crippled world. As your parents held you, I watched. I was with you. I watched you grow; I heard your laughter and cries, and I also saw the shortcomings of those around you. As you grew up, I felt your loneliness, and My heart longed to console you and remind you that I was with you. I wanted to tell you that I had not abandoned you. But you had forgotten Me, and no one told you about Me and My love for you. Because of the free will I had given, I could only watch the mistakes of those around you, so I stood beside you, loving you. You had been pulled down in a broken world, but this suffering was going to bear life. As your life was taken from you, and decisions were made for you, do not doubt My presence beside you. I was going to redeem you; that was always the plan though you couldn't remember it. You were going to be My beacon of light. I was with you.

Life with its brokenness was kicking and beating you up. You fell, exhausted; you bought the lies, and started to live out of your wounds and fears. Lashing out in pain, screaming in agony, you entered into the Darkness. The ones who should have loved and protected you betrayed you. I know the pain of betrayal and abandonment. I saw you fall under the weight. As you gave up under the weight that sin had placed upon your shoulders, I wept for you. My child. I was with you.

As Satan infected everything around you to cause you torment, and to sow seeds of future torment, My eyes never left you. He wanted to destroy you. You couldn't see the landmines he was laying for you, but as I watched, I knew that the greater the Darkness he created, the brighter I would lead you to shine. The Darkness would not overcome the Light. My words, once spoken, would not return empty.

So I allowed free will of those around you to reign, knowing it would all be used for My purpose. I was never away; I was with you. When Satan had completed all his works of Darkness, it was finally time. My heart, burning for love of you, could now pour its love out upon you. It was time for our reunion! You and I were going to meet again. I was going to remind you that you were Mine.

My Mother, the gentle Mother, came forth and said, "Son, allow me to talk to her first. Let me prepare her to meet You. The Darkness of the world has covered her, let me help clear the way in her heart and mind."

So, I waited patiently for my Mother to speak to you. I was so happy when you answered her call! I smiled as you responded to her voice! I was with you. Finally, it was time to visit you. I wondered if you would remember Me—My Mother wanted to come with Me so you wouldn't be afraid. That night when We came, I longed for you to recognize Me and rejoice, but your mind was filled with fear. So, we spoke to your soul, and your soul embraced Us in joy, and We shared Our love for you, and you shared everything you had carried over the forty years of separation. We clung to each other, and I reminded you of your work that you had said, "yes" to in heaven.

When you awoke, Satan took up his place in your mind and started arguing with you. But now your soul had been awakened, and your mind was no longer the dictator. The time had come for you to know Me and Satan was furious. He worked hard to scare you, but I was giving you the Grace to fight Fear. Your love for me was beginning to fight the attacks. I gave you all that you needed to break free from bondage, but you had to say, "yes." I never touched your free will. You could have rejected all the signs I was giving you and succumbed to the screaming voice of Satan. My Mother, my Father, and I watched.

I was with you.

Finally, the day came when you asked for Truth with an innocent and open heart, like a child. And, because there were no barriers, I was able to pour the Truth into your heart. Heaven watched, holding its breath. As you recognized and accepted Me with your free will, all of Heaven shook with joy and rejoicing. The celebration, the feast, had begun. One more soul had woken up and was united with Me and was now in the Heavenly Army.

My Father was joyful that a soul, a child He loved so much that He had sent His only begotten Son for, had been saved. Finally, He was able to meet His daughter. As all this happened, I was right beside you.

I know, my sweet child, that the road got rockier and unbearable after we were united, but understand that your love and faith in Me had to be tested, purified, cleansed, and strengthened. Satan helped Me do that, and to his anger and disgust, you stayed faithful to Me; you heeded My voice and promptings.

So today do you see this plan? This path that was allowed by Me, not to hurt you, but to use it as an opportunity to refine you—in fire, so you could truly be My Light to shine in the Darkness.

You have listened well to My voice, My daughter. Don't doubt now. Trust that it is Me, your Beloved, your Jesus, who is speaking to you. Just as I have not let a drop of your suffering be wasted, I will not let your present pain be for naught. I have come so you may have Life and have it abundantly. This is not a lie. People have forgotten, lost faith in My power, My miracles—I will show them.

My power is greater than the wiles of the Evil One. Just as I had a plan for your life, I have a plan for every Child of Mine. Ask them to come to Me like a child, and I will manifest My power, and they will see My Glory. I am the Alpha and the Omega, the Beginning and the End. All things came to be through Me and without Me, nothing came to be. I will conquer all. Have faith. Have peace. I am your Jesus.

I am with you, fear not."

As I surrendered myself in this final dance in my Beloved's arms, I knew I was at last dancing the ultimate dance of my life.

> *"'Arise, my darling, my beautiful one, and come along.*
> *For behold, the winter is past,*
> *The rain is over and gone.*
> *The flowers have already appeared in the land;*
> *The time has arrived for pruning the vines,*
> *And the voice of the turtledove has been heard in our land.*
> *The fig tree has ripened its figs,*
> *And the vines in blossom have given forth their fragrance.*
> *Arise, my darling, my beautiful one,*
> *And come along!'"*

> *– Song of Solomon 2:10-13*

EPILOGUE

"To fall in love with God is the greatest romance; to seek him the greatest adventure; to find him, the greatest human achievement."

– St. Augustine of Hippo

Nine years have passed since I first heard the sweet and gentle voice of Mary that led me into the greatest adventure of my life. Looking back, it seems like yesterday that I heard Mary's whisper, and all the dreams and experiences are as vivid and clear as the first day. During this time, my life has changed more than I could have imagined. Along the way, I formed some of the closest friendships, and been blessed by the wisdom of holy priests. I have been able to face some of the most challenging times where my faith has been tested, and I have had to make a choice once again.

In choosing Jesus, I have found myself standing alone in the darkness holding on to Jesus. I have now come to realize life is an ongoing journey where such decisions will have to be made, and usually at a high cost. Accepting Jesus as Lord was just the beginning. I would have to prove that continuously, and the enemy has not missed any opportunity to challenge my faith. However, God has made known His presence and His love to me through the unwavering support and prayers of holy people He has brought into my life. This has allowed me to walk through the storms with my integrity, dignity, and faith intact.

I have received a new name, "Nikki", to match my new identity. Since my conversion, I had felt like a new creation and believed in my heart that God would give me a new name. Seven years later He did. He spoke through a friend who suddenly started calling me "Nikki" and couldn't explain why. When I heard it for the first time I immediately knew that this was the new name that I had been waiting for, as it felt right and there was a familiarity to it.

Encountering Jesus has radically changed my perspective on life. As a Muslim in America, I believed I was finally living in freedom, but in reality I was living in bondage. Being a sinner, I carried a heavy burden and lived under God's justice. This burden was taken off my shoulders when I accepted Jesus as my Lord and Savior. He took the punishment of my sins upon Himself and set me free from God's judgment. Through accepting Jesus as my Redeemer, I entered into God's mercy. I realize that a person can live in a country like America and be physically free, but still be a prisoner spiritually. I know today that a person could live in an oppressive culture but still be spiritually free, and sadly also live in a free culture and still be in spiritual bondage.

I am grateful to God for giving me both physical and spiritual freedom. It truly has been a gift from God for I certainly did nothing to deserve it. We cannot do anything to earn God's mercy and love; He offers it to us as a gift. It is perfectly said in Romans 5:8, "But God proves His love for us in that while we were still sinners Christ died for us" and of course the much quoted verse from John 3:16 "For God so loved the world that He gave His only begotten Son, so that everyone who believes in him might not perish but might have eternal life."

Jesus gave His life for all mankind, but the graces that flow from that sacrifice are only efficacious to those who accept it. It is a River of Living Water that flows within reach of every person, but only those who bend their knee and drink from it receive the salvation and eternal life.

I have shared my journey with the personal and mystical events to explain how I came into a relationship with the Father. If some of you struggle to understand or believe it, I hope you will at least consider the possibility. My purpose is not to convince you to believe it, but I hope to awaken a desire in your heart to search deeper for the truth, and without giving God boundaries to respond within. When He speaks to you, which I am sure He will, don't let your mind attack you with fear and arguments, and hijack the greatest adventure and love story of your life.

To those who believe in Jesus, I hope that reading my story has affirmed your faith. Jesus is not a historical figure, but the resurrected Lord who wants a relationship with each one of us. People may think I am special because I have had these experiences. But God's love for us is so great that He is speaking worldwide to the most closed hearts like mine in very personal ways. There are many reports of Jesus appearing to thousands of Muslims in similar ways. But we always retain our free will and have a choice to accept or deny Him. I too had a choice, as I could have easily written off the dreams and whispers as a creation of my mind or a visit from the Prophet Isa. I had to take every step of the way for God never touched my free will.

It is easy to miss the soft and gentle voice of God, as the noise around us is so loud. Or, when we do hear the whisper, we are not agreeable to what we are hearing, or doubt that God would really speak to us. So we choose to write it off as just a figment of our imagination. Therefore, we sadly miss the treasures of these God moments that would help sustain us in the difficult times.

God may be speaking to you and maybe prompting you to do something today. If you listen and follow His promptings, you will be surprised how much more He will speak once He has your attention! Our relationship with God can only blossom in the fertile soil of faith and trust. So, if you hear His voice, harden not your hearts (Psalm 95:8).

I thank you for taking this journey with me through my life, and I leave you with the most important question: Jesus is the Savior of the world, but is He your personal Savior? Do you believe He died for your salvation?

Recently during the consecration at Mass, as the priest was reciting the prayers, I saw myself at Calvary. I was alone, and Jesus was being stretched out on the cross, and His eyes met mine, and I felt Him say that this was just for me. He was going to allow the nails to be driven into His hands and feet because I was so precious to Him. He was dying to save me. I wanted to run to stop Him! But my eyes met His, and I fell silent. I realized that the weight of my sins was so heavy that I couldn't be saved without His sacrifice. Justice had to be done, the price of sin had to be paid, and I was incapable of paying it. It had to be this way. At the foot of the Cross, I accepted the greatest gift, the gift of personal redemption. Jesus Christ is the only one who offers this gift of salvation.

The Lord then took me deeper into this mystery. I invite you to place yourself at the foot of the Cross as you read the following meditation. Let Him speak to your heart. If you already know Him, may you come to an even deeper union. But if you do not, I encourage you to open your heart with childlike trust, and let Him reveal the Truth to you. May you encounter Him in a personal way and become a new creation in Christ Jesus!

"You see, My Child; it had to be this way. You were sinking in the swamp of your sins. The more you struggled, the more you sank. You were surrounded by others who were sinking, as well, and they grabbed onto you and pushed you down so they could stay up. This was your world, My Child, so I had to come for you, you were My Beloved Child, and I couldn't bear to leave you in Darkness. God's justice had to be done; the wages of sin had to be paid. So, with My eyes upon you, I went to the Cross. I offered Myself, willingly as ransom so you could be freed. As I looked upon you with love, I was able to bear the scourges laid upon me.

When I saw you lost and sinking, I was able to stretch My hands on that Cross and stay there as they nailed Me. As I saw the Darkness choking you, I was able to breathe My last and offer it to My Father so that you might be saved.

So, you see, My Child, it had to be. I died for you, so you could be saved.

As the price of sin was paid on the Cross, the wages of sin were paid, your feet suddenly found solid ground. No longer were you sinking as you stood catching your breath, you finally looked around and saw the Darkness surrounding you, the hands wanting to grab and pull you down. These faces were familiar, loved by you, and they called out to you to be with them.

At that moment, My Child, you had to make the most-important decision...choose to be saved or join the familiar faces in the Darkness.

I watched you, and I wondered how it was going to be—would you turn to Me or go back? Would you accept the Redemption that I had won with My Blood that was being offered to you? You turned away from the Darkness and chose to look at the source of firm ground under your feet. You turned towards Love, searching for Light. I had laid a path out for you that would lead you out of the swamp towards Me. You saw the path; you knew it would be a path you would walk alone. Every step you had a choice. Every step I waited, wanting you to take the next step towards Me.

You have walked well, My Child. You stand on solid ground, but you have to keep taking that next step towards Me. There are still dangers along the path, but if you choose Me every step, you will do well. I have laid the path for you with My Blood. Follow Me to My Father's House where I wait for you. Every step, accept My sacrifice for you, and you will see the marks of My Blood guiding you Home.

So, you see, My Child, it had to be. I died for you, so you could be saved.

As the price of sin was paid on the Cross, the wages of sin were paid, your feet suddenly found solid ground. No longer were you sinking as you stood catching your breath, you finally looked around and saw the Darkness surrounding you, the hands wanting to grab and pull you down. These faces were familiar, loved by you, and they called out to you to be with them.

At that moment, My Child, you had to make the most-important decision...choose to be saved or join the familiar faces in the Darkness.

I watched you, and I wondered how it was going to be—would you turn to Me or go back? Would you accept the Redemption that I had won with My Blood that was being offered to you? You turned away from the Darkness and chose to look at the source of firm ground under your feet. You turned towards Love, searching for Light. I had laid a path out for you that would lead you out of the swamp towards Me. You saw the path; you knew it would be a path you would walk alone. Every step you had a choice. Every step I waited, wanting you to take the next step towards Me.

You have walked well, My Child. You stand on solid ground, but you have to keep taking that next step towards Me. There are still dangers along the path, but if you choose Me every step, you will do well. I have laid the path for you with My Blood. Follow Me to My Father's House where I wait for you. Every step, accept My sacrifice for you, and you will see the marks of My Blood guiding you Home.

Your Savior and Friend,
Jesus

Thirst
for Truth

FROM MOHAMMAD TO JESUS

DISCUSSION GUIDE FOR READING GROUP

DISCUSSION QUESTIONS

1. Nikki's visit to St. Patrick's Cathedral commenced her journey towards Christ. Is there a place you have visited that brought about a spiritual awakening, or a turning point in your faith?

2. Nikki describes her conversion to Christianity as a rebirth. With this rebirth came a desire for a new name--one to reflect her new identity in Christ. Have you experienced a conversion, or reconversion of faith that has changed you, and your perspective on life?

3. Coming to terms with the identity of Jesus was a central struggle for Nikki. Was He the Messiah or a Prophet? With this question in mind, who is Jesus to you? Is He the living Messiah who is part of your daily life, or is He kept within historical boundaries? Why should these different roles matter? Why might one want to reflect on them?

4. In Chapter 12, The Search, Nikki describes her encounter with God and when she was told to "come back like a child." What has been your experience in seeking His voice? What represents your greatest challenge to hearing His voice?

5. The central point in the book is Nikki's quest for objective Truth and how her life changed after encountering it. How do you understand Truth? Do you feel it is necessary to discern and follow Truth in all situations and do you believe it comes with a cost? Give any examples of a time you had to make such a choice.

6. Nikki's conversion shows how God is personally involved in each person's life and nothing is impossible for Him. Reflecting on your own life, can you give examples of how God has surprised you beyond your expectations, or how you overcame seemingly impossible situations?

About the Author

Nikki Kingsley savors the freedom and faith that she has found in her new home in the United States. Her dream of providing free choices, and opportunities for her two children was realized as both have become Christians, graduated from college, and successfully forged their own unique and independent paths.

Nikki gives talks about her journey and conversion with a spiritual sensitivity. She shares life lessons of her faith—learned through her search for Truth. Nikki Kingsley continues to write, and speak sharing her message and offering hope to various audiences.

Ms. Kingsley's interviews on radio stations include: EWTN, Immaculate Heart, Sirius, Ava Maria, and The Catholic Channel. She has spoken at various businesses, conferences and parish groups across the United States.

To invite Nikki to speak at your event or to do a book signing, please visit:

www.nikkikingsley.com.

Nikki Kingsley may be contacted at:

nikki@nikkikingsley.com.

THIS BOOK MAY BE PURCHASED AT
NIKKIKINGSLEY.COM